Canada's Residential Schools

Volume 3

Canada's Residential Schools:
The Métis Experience

The Final Report of the
Truth and Reconciliation
Commission of Canada

Volume 3

Published for the
Truth and Reconciliation Commission

by

McGill-Queen's University Press
Montreal & Kingston • London • Chicago

2015

Truth and Reconciliation Commission of Canada

Website: www.trc.ca

ISBN 978-0-7735-4655-4 (v. 3 : bound).   ISBN 978-0-7735-4656-1 (v. 3 : paperback).

Printed in Canada on acid-free paper

An index to this volume of the final report is available online. Please visit http://nctr.ca/trc_reports.php

Library and Archives Canada Cataloguing in Publication
Truth and Reconciliation Commission of Canada
[Canada's residential schools]
    Canada's residential schools : the final report of the Truth and Reconciliation Commission of Canada.

(McGill-Queen's Native and northern series ; 80–86)
Includes bibliographical references and index.
Contents: v. 1. The history. Part 1, origins to 1939 — The history. Part 2, 1939 to 2000 — v. 2. The Inuit and
    northern experience — v. 3. The Métis experience — v. 4. The missing children and unmarked burials
    report — v. 5. The legacy — v. 6. Reconciliation

Issued in print and electronic formats.
ISBN 978-0-7735-4649-3 (v. 1, pt. 1 : bound).   ISBN 978-0-7735-4650-9 (v. 1, pt. 1 : paperback).
ISBN 978-0-7735-4651-6 (v. 1, pt. 2 : bound).   ISBN 978-0-7735-4652-3 (v. 1, pt. 2 : paperback).
ISBN 978-0-7735-4653-0 (v. 2 : bound).   ISBN 978-0-7735-4654-7 (v. 2 : paperback).
ISBN 978-0-7735-4655-4 (v. 3 : bound).   ISBN 978-0-7735-4656-1 (v. 3 : paperback).
ISBN 978-0-7735-4657-8 (v. 4 : bound).   ISBN 978-0-7735-4658-5 (v. 4 : paperback).
ISBN 978-0-7735-4659-2 (v. 5 : bound).   ISBN 978-0-7735-4660-8 (v. 5 : paperback).
ISBN 978-0-7735-4661-5 (v. 6 : bound).   ISBN 978-0-7735-4662-2 (v. 6 : paperback).
ISBN 978-0-7735-9817-1 (v. 1, pt. 1 : ePDF).   ISBN 978-0-7735-9818-8 (v.1, pt. 1 : ePUB).
ISBN 978-0-7735-9819-5 (v. 1, pt. 2 : ePDF).   ISBN 978-0-7735-9820-1 (v. 1, pt. 2 : ePUB).
ISBN 978-0-7735-9821-8 (v. 2 : ePDF).   ISBN 978-0-7735-9822-5 (v. 2 : ePUB).
ISBN 978-0-7735-9823-2 (v. 3 : ePDF).   ISBN 978-0-7735-9824-9 (v. 3 : ePUB).
ISBN 978-0-7735-9825-6 (v. 4 : ePDF).   ISBN 978-0-7735-9826-3 (v. 4 : ePUB).
ISBN 978-0-7735-9827-0 (v. 5 : ePDF).   ISBN 978-0-7735-9828-7 (v. 5 : ePUB).
ISBN 978-0-7735-9829-4 (v. 6 : ePDF).   ISBN 978-0-7735-9830-0 (v. 6 : ePUB)

1. Native peoples—Canada—Residential schools. 2. Native peoples—Education—Canada.
3. Native peoples—Canada—Government relations. 4. Native peoples—Canada—Social conditions.
5. Native peoples—Canada—History. I. Title. II. Series: McGill-Queen's Native and northern series ; 80–86

E96.5.T78 2016   971.004'97   C2015-905971-2
                                            C2015-905972-0

Contents

Canada's Residential Schools

Volume 3

Introduction

The central goal of the Canadian residential school system was to 'Christianize' and 'civilize' Aboriginal people, a process intended to lead to their cultural assimilation into Euro-Canadian society. This policy goal was directed at all Aboriginal people and all Aboriginal cultures. It failed to take into account the development of new Aboriginal nations, and the implications of the *Indian Act*'s definition of who was and was not a "status Indian" and the *British North America Act*'s division of responsibility for "Indians." In the government's vision, there was no place for the Métis Nation that proclaimed itself in the Canadian Northwest in the nineteenth century. Neither was there any place for the large number of Aboriginal people who, for a variety of reasons, chose not to terminate their Treaty rights, or for those women, and their children, who lost their *Indian Act* status by marrying a person who did not have such status. These individuals were classed or identified alternately as "non-status Indians," "half-breeds," or "Métis." In different times or different places, they might also identify themselves by these terms, but often they did not. Instead, they might view themselves to be members of specific First Nations, Inuit, or Euro-Canadian societies. For the sake of clarity, this chapter generally uses the term *Métis* to describe people of mixed descent who were not able, or chose not, to be registered as Indians under the *Indian Act*. It should be recognized that not all the people described by this term would have identified themselves as Métis during their lives, and that the histories of these people varied considerably, depending on time and location.

Canada's residential school system was a partnership between the federal government and the churches. When it came to the Métis, the partners had differing agendas. Since the churches wished to convert as many Aboriginal children (and, indeed, as many people) as possible, they had no objection to admitting Métis children to the boarding schools they established in the nineteenth century. Métis children were, for example, among the first students enrolled at the school at Fort Providence in the Northwest Territories.[1] Métis children were also in many of the mission schools that were established by the Oblates throughout the West.[2] In one case, the presence of Métis children at Catholic missions was a matter of disappointment. French-born

Oblate Adrien-Gabriel Morice came to Canada in the 1880s in the hope of working with 'exotic Indians,' only to find that the students at the Mission, British Columbia, school were Métis.[3] The churches never dropped their interest in providing residential schooling to Métis children. The Anglicans, for example, opened hostels for Métis children in the Yukon in the 1920s and the 1950s, and in Alberta, Catholic-owned residential schools maintained a high enrolment of Métis students.

The federal government policy on providing schooling to Métis children was conflicted. It viewed the Métis as members of the 'dangerous classes,' whom the residential schools were intended to civilize and assimilate. This view led to the adoption of policies that allowed for the admission of Métis children at various times. However, from a jurisdictional perspective, the federal government believed that the responsibility for educating and assimilating Métis people lay with provincial and territorial governments. There was a strong concern that if the federal government began providing funding for the education of some of the children for whom the provinces and territories were responsible, it would find itself having to take responsibility for the rest.[4] When this view dominated, Indian agents would be instructed to remove Métis students from residential schools.

Despite their perceived constitutional responsibility, provincial and territorial governments were reluctant to provide services to Métis people. They did not ensure that there were schools in Métis communities, or work to see that Métis children were admitted and welcomed into the public school system. Many Métis parents who wished to see their children educated in schools had no option but to try to have them accepted into a residential school. In some cases, these would be federally funded schools, but in other cases, Métis students attended church-run schools or residences that did not receive federal funding.

As provincial governments slowly began to provide increased educational services to Métis students after the Second World War, Métis children lived in residences and residential schools that were either run or funded by provincial governments. The Métis experience is an important reminder that the impact of residential schools extends beyond the formal residential school program that Indian Affairs operated. The history of these provincial schools and the experiences of Métis students in these schools remain to be written.[5]

The existing records make it impossible to say how many Métis children attended residential school. But they did attend almost every residential school discussed in this report at some point. They would have undergone the same experiences—the high death rates, limited diets, crowded and unsanitary housing, harsh discipline, heavy workloads, neglect, and abuse—described in the other volumes of this history.

Métis people not only were educated in the schools, but they also, on occasion, played a role in their operation. Angélique and Marguerite Nolin, two Métis sisters who had been born in Sault Ste. Marie and educated by the Sisters of Charity in

Montréal, opened a school at Red River in 1829. In 1834, the Nolins travelled to the parish of Baie St. Paul in what is now Manitoba, where they helped establish a school for First Nations and Métis.[6] Henry Budd, James Settee, James Hope, and Charles Pratt, four of the prominent graduates of the Anglican boarding school at Red River in the early nineteenth century, all went on to become missionaries and teachers.[7] In the 1860s, Louis Riel was one of a number of young Métis who were sent to study at the Catholic schools of Lower Canada.[8] In the 1880s, Riel taught at a boarding school for Métis boys in Montana.[9] Riel's sister Sara was educated at the Sisters of Charity boarding school at Red River. After taking her vows in 1868, she became a teacher at the Île-à-la-Crosse boarding school.[10] Anglican schools at Red River also enrolled children of mixed ancestry.

This document focuses on those elements of the residential school history that were unique to Métis people. As such, the discussion centres on government and church policy regarding enrolment, and on the history of a number of institutions that were primarily intended for Métis students. The conclusion brings the focus back to the students, making use of statements that have been given to the Truth and Reconciliation Commission of Canada, and of several projects that collected Métis residential school memories. One of the most significant of these is the Métis Nation of Alberta's *Métis Memories of Residential Schools*: *A Testament to the Strength of the Métis*.

CHAPTER 1

Student lives

To demonstrate the variety and complexity of the Métis residential school experience, we start with the story of three former students. These stories demonstrate that there was no single route for Métis children into residential schools, or a single experience. For Madeline Bird, the school served as a child-welfare facility when crisis struck her family. Maria Campbell's family was split over the decision to place her in a residential school. Her stay in a residential school was brief and unpleasant, but, as her memoir makes clear, the public schools that she attended treated her and her siblings in a racist and humiliating fashion. James Gladstone attended both a boarding school and an industrial school. He was subject to disease, witnessed the death of a friend that he attributed to inadequate medical attention, and spent much of his time at school doing chores or working in the school's print shop. Ironically, residential schooling contributed to a strengthening of his Aboriginal identity. He learned Aboriginal languages and cultural traditions from other boys, and, later, he would play a leadership role in Canadian Aboriginal life, eventually serving in the Canadian Senate. These stories only hint at the intricacy of the Métis residential school story.

Madeline Bird was born Madeline Mercredi on Potato Island near Fort Chipewyan in what is now Alberta in 1899. Her parents were Métis, her father having come from Manitoba.[1] Her mother, Julienne Laviolette, was from Fort Chipewyan, and had gone to the Fort Chipewyan school. "She was strict just like the sisters. Sometimes she was even stricter but she loved us a lot. As sick as I was, when I was young, she spanked me once in a while."[2] When Madeline's father, Joseph, died in 1909, one of her sisters was taken to Fort Vermilion, Alberta, by an uncle, her godfather. There, she was educated in the convent by the Sisters of Providence, and she returned to Fort Chipewyan when she was eighteen.[3] Madeline stayed in Fort Chipewyan, where she was raised in the Holy Angels school (which also served as a convent). A sickly child, she lived at the convent school until she was eighteen. Without the support of the nuns, she said, she did not believe she would have survived.[4] "There were lots of pitiful kids in those days. The orphans were more pitiful than everybody else because they were badly treated by the people and even by the relatives sometimes. The grandmothers were the best people to love and care for the orphans but the others they just starved and beat them, too often."[5]

Although most of the Métis at Fort Chipewyan spoke French, instruction at the school in the early twentieth century was in English one day and French the next. According to Bird, in her extended family, "no one wanted to speak English."[6] Schooling was largely confined to copying and memory work. "The sisters were not really teachers but they did their best. Some of them were very good teachers and were very good to us. Some just gave us a book and made us copy and copy so we became good writers. We copied for hours at a time, in silence."

Pens, pencils, and even paper were in limited supply. "Some sisters made us write with pencils because it was too hard to write with the old pen and nibs dipped in the ink bottle. It was a promotion for us to be able to write with the old-time pens. Then we had to erase everything we wrote so that we would have more paper to do some more copying."[7]

When they were not studying, they were working. "We had to haul in wood for the fire just like the boys and do all kinds of chores about our playrooms and dormitories and the playgrounds. We all had jobs to do. There were chores to do like washing dishes and the tables, sweeping floors in the playrooms, the sleeping rooms, the classrooms, the stairs and the hallways."[8]

Bird was proud of the skills she developed at the school.

> I learned everything in the convent, cooking bread, pastry and good meals,
> how to make butter, milk the cows and look after the chickens, how to do heavy
> laundry, decorate the altars, do bead work, crochet, knitting, crafts and quilting.
> I always tried to learn everything. I was like a jack of all trades and I tried to do
> everything good.[9]

There were so few staff members that the students were called upon to help in times of sickness.

> When a kid was too sick they had to stay in the infirmary and someone use [sic]
> to stay with them. Even me, I use [sic] to sit beside them when they were sick.
> That was hard on us because we were scared and sometimes they cried and were
> afraid they might die. The sisters were too busy and too few so they could not
> stay a long time with one kid.[10]

During one epidemic, Bird thought, the sisters could hardly have slept. "When everybody was in bed, the sisters carried up big jars of hot drinks for the kids to drink and prevent sickness and complications."[11]

A variety of rules were in place to guard the students' morals. Bird could recall getting in trouble for whistling. "They use [sic] to say that I was calling the devil."[12] Permission was required to attend weddings and funerals in the local Anglican church.[13] And, when one girl wrote a letter to a newly arrived Oblate brother, she was quickly expelled at the insistence of the bishop, even though she was an orphan with "no money and no place to go."[14]

While her memoir often describe the nuns and priests of Fort Chipewyan as being strict, her overall assessment was one of gratitude and understanding. She credited them with saving her life and teaching her all she knew—in both practical and spiritual terms.[15] She also thought their lives were as hard and difficult as those of the students.

> After working all day they slept in the dormitories with the kids. They didn't even have their own rooms, just big white curtains like a small white square around their beds. They could hear everything all night and got up to take care of the kids who cried because they were sick, cold, or had a bad dream.... Some of them came from schools and homes where they saw lots of meanness and punishments. They thought that was the best way. They got scolded badly by their Superiors, too, when the kids did wrong, so they had to be strict.[16]

Maria Campbell was born in 1940 into a Métis family that had fled to Spring River, "fifty miles [80.4 kilometres] north-west of Prince Albert," after the North-West Rebellion of 1885. The community members had originally made their living as hunters and trappers. When the land was opened to homesteading in the 1920s, many of them attempted to farm in an effort to hold on to at least a little land. Lacking both experience and capital, most were not able to fulfill the requirements to break a specified number of acres within three years. Their land was taken over by new settlers, and they retreated to shacks on road allowances, the thirty-foot-wide (nine-metre) strips of government-owned land on either side of a road.[17] Despite the ever-present poverty, Campbell's was a literate household. Her mother read to the children from the works of "Shakespeare, Dickens, Sir Walter Scott," and the poet Henry Wadsworth Longfellow.[18] Her grandmother Dubuque had Treaty status and had been raised in a convent, and one of her great-grandmothers, Cheechum, was related to Métis military leader Gabriel Dumont.[19] The family members were regular Catholic churchgoers. "The Mass was held in Latin and French, and sometimes in Cree. The colourful rituals were the only thing which made the church bearable for me. I was spellbound by the scarlets and purples and even the nuns, whom I disliked as persons, were mystical and haunting in their black robes with huge, swinging crosses."[20]

Campbell's life underwent a dramatic change when she was seven. One evening at dinner, Grannie Dubuque announced that she had arranged a special surprise for Maria: she had been accepted into the residential school at Beauval, Saskatchewan.

> It sounded exciting, but looking at Dad's shocked face, Mom's happy one, and Cheechum's stony expression—a sure sign of anger—I was confused. Dad went out after dinner and did not return until the next day. Meanwhile Momma and Grannie planned my wardrobe. I remember only the ugly black stockings, woolly and very itchy, and the little red tam I had to wear and how much I hated it.[21]

Of her year at Beauval, she recalled little except loneliness and fear.

> The place smelled unpleasantly of soap and old women, and I could hear my
> footsteps echoing through the building. We prayed endlessly, but I cannot recall
> ever doing much reading or school-work as Momma had said I would—just the
> prayers and my job, which was cleaning the dorms and hallways. I do recall most
> vividly a punishment I once received. We weren't allowed to speak Cree, only
> French and English, and for disobeying this, I was pushed into a small closet
> with no windows or light, and locked in for what seemed like hours. I was almost
> paralyzed with fright when they came to let me out. I remember the last day of
> school and the sense of freedom I felt when Dad came for me. He promised that
> I would never have to go back, as a school was being built at home.[22]

She quickly discovered that the public school was not a very welcoming place for
Métis students. Campbell's classroom was divided by race, with Euro-Canadians on
one side and Métis on the other. Campbell recalled that "we had a lot of fights with the
white kids, but finally, after beating them soundly, we were left alone."[23] Mealtimes
underscored the differences between the two groups of students.

> They had white or brown bread, boiled eggs, apples, cakes, cookies, and jars of
> milk. We were lucky to have these even at Christmas. We took bannock for lunch,
> spread with lard and filled with wild meat, and if there was no meat we had cold
> potatoes and salt and pepper, or else whole roasted gophers with sage dressing.
> No apples or fruit, but if we were lucky there was a jam sandwich for dessert.[24]

One of the teachers alternated between bursts of cruelty, often ridiculing Métis
children for their errors, followed by guilty gestures of kindness.[25]

At one point, Campbell, overcome by shame about her ancestry, went home and
called her parents "no-good Halfbreeds." Her great-grandmother walked her away
from the house. Then, after talking with her about her attitude, she beat Campbell and
told her, "I will beat you each time I hear you talk as you did. If you don't like what you
have, then stop fighting your parents and do something about it yourself." Then she
walked her back home.[26]

James Gladstone, a future Canadian senator, attended both St. Paul's, the Anglican
boarding school on the Blood Reserve, and the Calgary Industrial School in Alberta in
the early twentieth century. Born in 1887, he was raised at Mountain Mill near Pincher
Creek, in what is now Alberta, by his grandparents, Harriet and William Gladstone.
William, a non-Aboriginal man, had been born in Montréal in 1832 and worked in
the North American West from 1848 onwards. He married Harriet Leblanc, a Cree
woman, in 1855. Many of their children became Catholics, but William Gladstone
remained a staunch Protestant throughout his life. One of their daughters, also named
Harriet, lived with a non-Aboriginal man, James Bowes, for a number of years. She
gave birth to four children, one of whom was James Gladstone. Because James's father

was non-Aboriginal, James grew up without status under the *Indian Act*. Despite this, he attended two residential schools. His presence in those schools is clear evidence of the fact that, despite shifting government policy on funding and admission, many non-status children attended residential schools.

In 1894, James's cousin Nellie was taking her brother Alex to the Roman Catholic residential school at High River, in what is now Alberta. Hoping that he might become Catholic, she decided to enrol seven-year-old James in the school as well. Even though she had no permission from either James's parents or grandparents, she was able to get both boys admitted to the school. But James's stay at the school was short-lived. As soon as he saw his cousin drive her wagon away from the school ground, he realized that he wanted to go home. At first running after his cousin's wagon, he soon realized he would not be able to catch up on foot, and he began a days-long journey, catching rides with train gangs when he could, and finally meeting up with his cousin on the final leg of the route home.

His grandfather William was determined that James would not fall into Catholic hands again. James's lack of status under the *Indian Act* should have been a barrier to his admission to the Anglican St. Paul's boarding school on the Blood Reserve. His grandfather, however, made use of his friendship with local rancher F. W. Godsal, a financial benefactor of the school, to gain admission for both James and his brother Steven.[27]

On his arrival at the school, Gladstone could speak English and Cree, but not Blackfoot, which was the language spoken by most of the students at the school. At first, he was able to communicate with his fellow students through a sign language that was familiar to Aboriginal people across the Prairies.[28] Gladstone stayed at the school for six years. While he was there, he learned to speak Blackfoot and absorbed a great deal of Blackfoot culture.[29] In a memoir of his days at the school, Gladstone wrote, "In those days, the teachers were dedicated to their work. They used to urge us to speak English and those who were on their best behaviour got five, ten or fifteen cents on Saturday. This money came from the teacher's own pocket. I remember I was punished several times for speaking Blackfoot."[30]

In 1899, the school discharged the Gladstone boys because of issues with their status. Steven returned home, but twelve-year-old James remained on the reserve, living at the home of an Anglican missionary and working for him as a translator, while attending a school for the children of Indian Affairs staff.[31] In 1900, after considerable discussions between Ottawa and the local Indian agent, Gladstone was readmitted to the school as a resident of the Blood Reserve. Under this arrangement, the federal government would be paying for the cost of his education.[32]

Gladstone was critical of the medical care available to the students. In the spring of 1900, a fellow student, Joe Glasgow, became ill after stepping on a nail. "Rev. Owen had made arrangements for a doctor from Fort Macleod, but he was a useless drunk who didn't come until it was too late. I looked after Joe for two days until he died. I was the only one he would listen to during his delirium."[33]

In 1903, he transferred to the Calgary Industrial School—over the objections of his principal. He went to Calgary to learn carpentry, but, since there was no carpentry instructor, he was put to work in the laundry and the kitchen. Eventually, he was put to work in the school print shop, which produced the magazine of the local Anglican diocese as well as other church-related publications. There, he trained as a typesetter and, according to his memoir, seldom went to classes.[34]

A student revolt was precipitated when a school laundress complained that a pair of her moccasins had disappeared. The principal put all the boys, including Gladstone, who was recovering from typhoid fever, on a bread-and-water diet until someone confessed to the theft. In protest, the students went on strike and took to begging for food in the streets of Calgary, returning to the school only to sleep. Eventually, twenty-five of them, including Gladstone, struck out for their homes. After walking forty kilometres, they stopped at a Cree camp, where the Mounted Police caught up with them. The police took them to the barracks at Okotoks and fed them, and the runaway boys organized a football game. The boys returned to the school by train the next day. Soon after their return, the laundress found the moccasins in her room under a stack of magazines.[35]

When he finished school, Gladstone returned to the Blood Reserve. In 1920, at the age of thirty-three, he was granted status under the *Indian Act*. He had married Janie Healy, a Kainai woman, and his application for status had the support of the local residential school principal, S. H. Middleton, the local Indian agent, and local First Nations leaders.[36]

CHAPTER 2

The Métis and the early residential school system: 1883–1910

In his 1879 report for the federal government, titled *Report on Industrial Schools for Indians and Half-Breeds*, Nicholas Flood Davin had proposed a central role in residential schooling and in assimilation in general for people of mixed descent, proclaiming them the "natural mediator between the Government and the red man, and also his natural instructor."[1] However, from the outset of the residential school system, there was opposition to extending residential schooling beyond 'Indians,' who were thought to be clearly a federal responsibility. On December 1, 1879, Hugh Richardson, a federal magistrate and member of the territorial council of the North-West Territories, living in Battleford,[2] advised the federal government that if "greater educational facilities" were provided to the Métis in the West without making the Métis pay for them, "the white population will, I think, have fairly just grounds to claim similar rights, and to grant this would not be practical at this time."[3] This view, which sought to exclude Métis children from residential schools in order to keep costs down, would remain a dominant factor in determining government policy.

In 1884, Father Joseph Hugonnard and Father Albert Lacombe, who were in the process of establishing the Qu'Appelle and High River schools, respectively, requested permission to admit the children of "white or half-breed" parents. While Lacombe suggested that the parents of the children might pay for their children's education at the school, Hugonnard did not. Indian Commissioner Edgar Dewdney opposed the application, saying that "we should keep the school for Indian children alone."[4] The following year, Lacombe was told he could admit Métis students as long their parents paid their costs—an almost insurmountable barrier for most parents.[5] In 1886, he was given permission to "admit a few Half-breed pupils to the school, for the purpose of endeavouring to induce the Indian children to remain at the school, as a sort of example to the Indian boys."[6] In the 1892–93 school year, the High River school admitted "six Half-breeds."[7]

During the system's first two decades, Métis students were in schools throughout the West. In 1889, when Principal J. R. Scott was recruiting students for the newly established Metlakatla industrial school in British Columbia, he travelled to a number of communities along the Nass River. "Eight Indians and four half-breed boys expressed their desire to enter the school. I told the latter I could not educate them; I, however, made an exception in favor of one of these."[8] This sort of exception became typical in the admission of students from families of mixed ancestry.

Because the federal government had established the industrial schools and provided most of their funding, the government had the authority to determine their admission policies. The missionaries retained greater control over who could be admitted to the smaller boarding schools. The boarding schools were generally church initiatives and received a lower level of federal funding than the industrial schools. As a result, the boarding schools were more likely to admit non-status children, although they had to pay for these students out of mission funds. In the early 1890s, most of the children at the Anglican boarding school at Onion Lake in what is now Saskatchewan were of mixed ancestry. Principal John Matheson taught the children at his own expense, only twice seeking government support in the form of food or a per capita grant.[9] In 1895, Matheson proposed a separate school for non-Treaty children at Onion Lake, which would operate in connection with the existing Anglican boarding school.[10] In 1898, he persuaded the government to pay the per capita grant for two children whose mother had status but whose Euro-Canadian father had deserted them. Indian Affairs warned Matheson that this was an isolated case and should not be considered as a precedent.[11] Two years later, only fourteen of the thirty-four students at the Anglican school at Onion Lake had Treaty status. At the Catholic school at the same location, forty-nine of the sixty-two students had status.[12] In 1897, in response to a Roman Catholic complaint that a Methodist principal was enrolling "non-Indian" students in British Columbia's Coqualeetza Institute, Indian agent Frank Devlin investigated. He found that 40 of 100 students were "non-Indians."[13]

According to the Department of Indian Affairs annual report for 1893, there were five "non-treaty Half-breeds" attending the Kamsack school as wards of the Presbyterian Church.[14] In 1895, Indian agent John Semmens was seeking direction on the enrolment of children of "mixed blood." He asked, "If the Father should be Indian and the mother White or vice versa could such children be admitted?"[15] When the Cluny, Alberta, school was inspected in 1898, of the thirty-five students at the school, thirteen did not have status under the *Indian Act*.[16]

During the 1880s and into the 1890s, missionaries put pressure on Indian Affairs to ensure that the children of "Half-Breeds" who had been "allowed to leave treaties" had access to schools.[17] The residential school principals were also alarmed by the number of Métis parents who were withdrawing from Treaty. With the numbered Treaties, Canada began requiring that Aboriginal people declare themselves to be either 'Indian' (and covered by Treaty), or 'Half-breed' and eligible for scrip (a certificate that could be exchanged for land or, later, for land or money). In some cases, individuals who had taken Treaty were allowed to withdraw from Treaty and claim scrip. Qu'Appelle principal Joseph Hugonnard worried in 1899, "Several half-breeds, belonging to the reserves, now taking treaty and classed as Indians, hope to withdraw and obtain 'scrip.'" Hugonnard noted that if many did so, they would have to take their children out of the school and "our attendance would be affected."[18] In May 1899, he wrote that there was a risk that the children of "Half-breeds" who were "related with or under the charge of treaty half-breeds" would become "a perpetual danger for educated Indians and the community" unless they were educated. For this reason, he wished to see them admitted to industrial schools.[19]

When Treaty 8 was negotiated in 1899—largely in response to the Yukon gold rush and the presence of prospectors in the area north of Great Slave Lake—Bishop Emile Grouard participated in the Treaty talks. Once the Treaty was negotiated, Grouard urged the Métis to take Treaty to ensure that their children would be eligible for federal funding while attending residential schools.[20]

The following year, Grouard wrote the prime minister to express his concern over the number of people of mixed ancestry who were withdrawing from Treaty. As a result, they were

> now in an infinitely inferior position to that of the other Indians, above all in regard to the education of their children. Until towns and villages are formed in this country, or settled establishments, no other school but a boarding school is possible. If the parents are nomads, at least their children may be reunited under the same roof and receive the benefits of instruction. It is this that the Government understands and which it wishes to bring about for the Indians. But these so-called halfbreeds, who are as nomadic as the Indians, who cannot help themselves to keep from being nomads, if they wish to live (for remember that we are not in the fertile plains of Alberta, but at Lake Athabaska and at the Great Slave Lake, every cultivation is practically impossible) what are they to do with their children? Who are not morally or physically distinguished from the Indian children. It seems to me that the only means to take are to permit us to, in this new country and under these exceptional circumstances which obtain there, receive in our boarding schools these halfbreed children on the same standard as the Indian children. Otherwise, as I have already explained to you, these unhappy halfbreed children will find themselves in a disastrously inferior position which will not produce any good result for the future.[21]

It was October of 1899 before Indian Affairs Minister Clifford Sifton outlined what would be the official policy on Métis and other non-status students for the next thirty-eight years. Sifton wrote that he could not agree with Indian Commissioner David Laird's proposal that "none but treaty children are to be admitted into Indian schools."

> A well-defined line can be drawn between halfbreeds, properly speaking and Indians. While I do not consider that the children of the halfbreeds proper of Manitoba and the Territories should be admitted into Indian schools and

paid for by the Department, I am decidedly of the opinion that all children, even those of mixed blood, whether legitimate or not, who live upon an Indian Reserve and whose parents on either side live as Indians upon a reserve, even if they are not annuitants, should be eligible for admission to the schools. It must be remembered that boarding and industrial schools were not established for the purpose of carrying out the terms of the treaty or complying with any provision of the law, but were instituted in the public interest, so that there should not grow up upon reserves an uneducated and barbarous class. The North West Government cannot provide for the education of non-annuitants upon reserves; and if we exclude them from our schools, they will practically be debarred from all means of education.[22]

Despite Sifton's pronouncement allowing the admission of Métis children to residential schools, government policy in coming years remained contradictory and haphazard. For example, during the early twentieth century, the federal government also provided limited support to an Oblate initiative that included a residential school for Métis students: the Saint-Paul-des-Métis colony.

Saint-Paul-des-Métis

In the 1890s, the Oblate missionary Albert Lacombe (the founding principal of the High River school) sought to create a Métis colony on the Canadian Prairies. Like many of the Oblates of this period, he was inspired in this endeavour by the Jesuit *reducciones* that had been established in Paraguay in the seventeenth century. In such a colony, Lacombe expected, the Oblates would provide education and agricultural training to the Métis, while maintaining a Catholic presence in an area into which a growing number of Protestant settlers were arriving.[23] He laid out his vision in an 1895 document entitled "A Philanthropic Plan to Redeem the Half-Breeds of Manitoba and the Northwest Territories." In it, he called on the federal government to set aside four townships of land in what is now Alberta for the colony. The land would be divided into forty-acre (sixteen-hectare) lots on which "the poor Half-breed families would be located." Lacombe recommended that "the head of family accepting the said 40 acres for his own use, and his heirs and successors, shall promise and sign a contract by which the title to the said land shall not be sold or alienated, but remain forever vested in the Crown." In addition, Lacombe asked that four sections of land be given to the Catholic Church "for the purpose of building a religious establishment and conducting thereon an Industrial School for Half-breed children."[24] The federal government agreed to lease two townships to the colony, which was to be administered by a board of management made up of the Catholic bishops of St. Boniface, St. Albert, and Prince Albert; Lacombe; and two of their appointees. Four sections of land were set aside on which the Catholic Church could erect "an Industrial School for Half-Breed Children." Two separate leases were established: one for the land for settlement and one for the land for the school and church. In both cases, the fee was $1 a year. In addition, the federal government agreed to provide up to $2,000 for the purchase of farm implements and seed "for the most needy of the half-breeds who may join the colony during the next financial year."[25] The land was north of the Saskatchewan River near the Egg and Saddle lakes in what is now Alberta.[26] Oblate Father Adéodat Thérien was appointed the resident manager.[27]

Lacombe then issued a call to the "Half-Breeds of Manitoba and the North-West," particularly those who "have no longer any home and do not know how to earn a living." The colony would have to start small, and could provide colonists with no financial aid. Lacombe promised that "as soon as possible, we shall establish industrial schools for boys and girls who shall be instructed in schooling and the various trades, chiefly in agricultural and cattle breeding."[28] The colony, which was to be known as Saint-Paul-des-Métis, commenced operations in the summer of 1896. On arrival, settlers were provided with eighty-acre (thirty-two-hectare) lots. By 1901, there were forty families in the colony. From the outset, it was plagued with funding problems and crop failures. The federal government declined to provide operating funding, as did the territorial government.[29]

In 1898, Thérien sought federal support for a residential school, pointing out that his attempts to establish a day school in the colony had failed. He wrote that "the settlers of the colony," being "more or less destitute," could not provide their children with clothing warm enough to protect them on the walk to and from school. Thérien recommended:

> Boarding schools should be erected wherein the Halfbreeds [sic] children could be kept and cared for, doing away thereby with the difficulties which hitherto have baffled our most strenuous efforts.

> The Halfbreeds themselves vividly realize the incapacity in which they are with regard the giving of a good education to their children and they strongly desire that boarding schools should be established and their children kept therein.

> From every part of the North-West, inquiries are made to that effect and attempt has been made on the part of the Halfbreeds to send their children to the boarding schools erected on the Indian Reserves. But as this scheme of sending the Halfbreed children to the Indian boarding schools cannot be adopted without great inconvenience the only way to solve the question would be to establish a boarding school exclusively for the Halfbreed children.[30]

Thérien requested a grant of $72 per student.[31] In lobbying Indian Affairs Minister Clifford Sifton for support for the school and the colony in general, Thérien portrayed the Métis as a potential social menace:

> A day will come and this day is nearer at hand than one would fancy, when the
> Government shall have to spend a large amount of money: to build jails and
> assure the security of law abiding citizen against the lawlessness of the poor,
> destitute half-breed rendered remorseless by the continuous spectacle of his
> poverty and self-degradation.[32]

Indian Affairs secretary H. C. Ross observed that although "in the North West
Territories the Dominion Government is responsible for the education of the people,"
the "half-breed children have no right to any favours in the matter of education."[33]
Lacombe renewed the call for school funding in the fall of that year. After inspecting
the colony in January 1899, Dominion Lands official A. A. Ruttan said that a boarding school "cannot be too soon established." However, Indian Affairs Deputy Minister
James Smart wrote at the time that there was "no chance at all" of the government's
funding such a project.[34]

In 1899, Thérien opened a boarding school that housed forty-eight students. It soon
was overcrowded, and, without federal support, the Oblates commenced construction
of a three-storey residential school that could accommodate between 100 and 150 students.[35] To address the colony's financial difficulties, Lacombe and Thérien undertook
fundraising campaigns throughout Canada and the United States in 1902 and 1903.
Canadian business leader Rodolphe Forget made a $5,000 donation, and the United
States railway executive, and former Canadian, James J. Hill donated another $5,000.[36]

The school, which had a capacity of over 100, opened in the fall of 1903.[37] It was
not popular with parents or their children. According to an account written in 1942
by Louis Guillaume, a member of the Oblate order who had worked in the colony, in
January 1905, several boys decided to burn down the school to retaliate for a punish-
ment they had been given. One of the older boys told the others that "if you want to get
rid of that prison, there was only one thing to do and that was to set fire to it."

Early in the morning of January 15, 1905, a fire was detected in the school. Although
the building was safely evacuated, one girl, Marguerite Ducharme, returned to the
building. She died in the blaze, which destroyed the entire school. The school
authorities concluded that the fire was arson. Initially, ten boys were taken into custody. A justice of the peace at Saddle Lake released four boys and sent others to Fort
Saskatchewan for trial. In an effort to frighten them, the police officer escorting them
on this journey told the boys that they were all likely to be hanged for their actions.
Terrified, the boys ran away, but were quickly recaptured.[38] James Macleod, a judge
of the Supreme Court of the North-West Territories and the former commissioner of
the North-West Mounted Police, heard the case.[39] During the trial, the defence law-
yer questioned whether anyone had died in the fire and, according to Guillaume's
account, "blamed the Rev. Sisters and the food." To Guillaume's surprise, the children were let go and the police officer who threatened them with hanging was given
a month in jail. Guillaume concluded, "Someone had probably worked to get those

children out of prison, under the pretext that there was no penitentiary in Edmonton and that they would have to be sent to Winnipeg. The children would have been lost forever."[40]

The fire marked the beginning of the end for the colony. Thérien became involved in efforts to increase immigration from Québec to the Prairies. It soon became apparent that Saint-Paul-des-Métis was to become a destination for these non-Métis settlers. In 1909, the colony was opened to general settlement. The attempt to establish a Métis colony had failed.[41]

CHAPTER 3

Forty years of haphazard policy:
1899–1937

Clifford Sifton's memorandum of 1899, which allowed the admission of students who did not have status under the *Indian Act* to residential schools, was often cited by Indian Affairs officials as the basis of the departmental policy on this issue. However, the policy was never clear and its implementation was far from consistent. A constant tension existed within government between a desire to control costs and a desire to control a perceived social menace. The first impulse favoured a restricted admissions policy; the second, a more open policy. The churches, struggling with difficulties in recruiting sufficient numbers of students, often viewed the enrolment of children of mixed descent as a way to fill their schools. In some cases, they were able to charge Métis parents a fee. In other cases, provincial governments paid them to accept students; and in yet others, the churches succeeded in having the federal government agree to pay for the education of non-status children.

Sifton's policy was not officially reversed until 1937, but there were times during this period when the federal government sought to reduce the enrolment of non-status children. Despite this, it is clear that during this period, Métis children were attending residential schools throughout the country. For example, in 1900, Indian Commissioner David Laird complained that Principal James Dagg "began rushing children into the Rupert's Land School with little regard as to whether they belonged to Treaty Indian families or not." Many of the students enrolled were not, in Laird's opinion, "entitled to the privilege."[1]

In 1905, the sister superior of the Roman Catholic school at Kenora, Ontario, asked Indian Affairs to provide grants to cover the expenses related to two "half-breed" orphan girls the church had admitted to the school "for charity's sake." The department turned down the request. The following year, Indian Affairs education official Martin Benson suggested that since the school's permitted enrolment had been increased from thirty to forty and the number had not been met, the department should consider providing a grant, on the condition that it should not be viewed as a precedent.[2] In January 1907, the department decided to receive the two children into Treaty, making them eligible for per capita support.[3] In explaining the decision in a memorandum to his minister, department official Duncan Campbell Scott wrote, "I have been accustomed to deal with cases of this nature upon grounds of humanity and expediency, rather than rules or regulations laid down by law, written or unwritten." He recommended that the children in question not only be accepted into the school, but also that they be taken into Treaty and made grant-earning students.[4]

Into the twentieth century, Onion Lake principal John Matheson continued to seek funding for "a large number of half-breeds and non-treaty children." He had been keeping them in the school at his own expense, but was having "difficulty in filling up his school with Indian children." The Indian commissioner ruled them not to be grant-earning students, saying that most of them were "orphans, children of Indian mothers by white or half-breed fathers, who deserted them. Mr Matheson says they are waifs and outcasts among the Indians and have none to care or provide for them and unless some institution takes them up they will undoubtedly form part of our criminal class." They were also "living on the reserve and brought up as Indians."[5]

By 1909, the High River, Alberta, school had a $1,500 deficit and was home to fifteen students who were not eligible for grants. Most of these non-grant-earning students were Métis children who had lost at least one parent.[6] The presence of Métis children at the High River school was highlighted in 1914 by Calgary newspaper reports of the complaints of a Métis woman. She had gone to the school and discovered that her children's feet were bruised and swollen, the result of having to do without boots for three months. Later that summer, a Saskatchewan lawyer, Arthur Burnett, wrote the department on behalf of a Métis man who complained that the principal would not let him take his children out of the school for the summer holiday. The man was distressed to discover his children were being poorly treated at the school. Indian Affairs official Duncan Campbell Scott asked Indian Commissioner W. A. Graham to investigate. Graham's response was mixed. He recognized that some Métis children were being kept against their parents' will, and they were sent home, but he was generally supportive of the school administration.[7]

In 1909, the government instructed some schools to discharge non-status students. This would have brought enrolment in the Methodist school in Red Deer, Alberta, down from forty-five to twenty-eight students (at a time when the approved enrolment was ninety). Not only would the numbers be a significant loss, the principal said, but also "some of the biggest and best trained boys and girls" were among the non-Treaty children. He said that "no quantity of new pupils could fill their place because all new pupils are young and untrained."[8] Duncan Campbell Scott informed the Methodist Missionary Society that the government, having no desire to see the Red Deer school close, was prepared to "wink" at the presence of Métis children in the school.[9] The following year, in his annual report, Scott pointed to the education of non-status children as one of the benefits of the residential school system.

> Not only are our schools every day removing intelligent Indian children from
> evil surroundings, but they are very often ministering to a class which would
> be outcasts without such aid; I refer to the illegitimate offspring of white men
> and Indian women who are thrown upon their mothers for support, and who
> have no legal status as Indians. This great charitable work, which parallels
> the efforts put forth by white communities, aided by provincial, municipal or
> private endowment, must be carried on by the Dominion government, aided by
> Christian missionaries and missionary societies.[10]

The 1910 contract between the federal government and the churches for the operation of residential schools addressed the issue of children of mixed descent, stipu-
lating that "no Half-breed children shall be admitted to the said school unless Indian
children cannot be obtained to complete the number authorized." Admission still
required the approval of the department, and no grant would be paid for any student
admitted under this provision.[11]

Indian Affairs departmental secretary J. D. McLean wrote the Saskatchewan minister of education in January 1911, outlining the new policy. His letter suggests that
the government was planning a much harsher approach than the contract stipu-
lated. According to McLean, "in future no half-breeds will be admitted to Boarding
or Industrial Schools conducted by this Department for the education of Indian children." However, he said there was no intention of dismissing any "half-breed" children currently in the schools.[12] The federal government was, ineffectually, attempting
to force provincial governments to take responsibility for Métis education.

In March 1911, Indian agents were instructed to "check carefully all applications
that come before you having particular reference to age and status of the appli-
cants."[13] Staff expressed differing views on the issue. The Indian agent at Battleford,
Saskatchewan, J. P. G. Day, wrote that the admission of non-Indian students would
reduce the overall standard of care in the school. He pointed out that

> when half-breed Children are admitted into a School as non-grant earners; there
> is very grave reason to believe that these Children are fed and clothed out of the
> per capita money Grant allowed by the Department for the other Pupils; and so
> they do not get the benefit they are entitled to, the School is also impaired in it's
> [sic] efficiency, which in turn helps to defeat the object for which the Schools are
> established, i.e. the education and improvement of our Indian Children, with the
> ultimate aim of fitting them to become self supporting, and good citizens.[14]

Indian Affairs school inspector J. A. J. McKenna opposed the policy. When faced
with the argument that it was the duty of the provinces to educate Métis students, he
reminded officials that "there are no Provincial institutions in which the same can
be provided, and that our Indian residential schools are the only existing agencies
for the proper up-bringing of the unfortunate class of children." In making this argument, he echoed Sifton's memorandum. What, he asked, was to prevent non-status

children "from becoming outcasts and menaces to society if they be not taken into Indian schools—schools established and maintained, be it remembered, not for the mere purpose of fulfilling the conditions of Indian treaties, but in the interest of the commonwealth."[15]

Despite the policy, school officials continued to enrol non-Treaty and mixed-ancestry students. In 1912, for instance, the principal of the Lestock, Saskatchewan, school reported, "Under the present arrangement, there is ample accommodation for 25 boys and 33 girls, with a staff of 10. So we took in 11 half-breed children and 1 Indian child under 7 years of age, besides the number on the roll."[16] It was reported that at High River, the "66 children recently admitted are given as half breeds." Frank Pedley, the Indian Affairs deputy minister, advised the minister, "The wholesale admission of the 66 Half-breeds to one Indian school is an indication of how extensively this work may be carried on if allowed to apply to the 19 industrial schools and the 54 boarding schools." The situation at High River was complicated by the fact that 290 students were reportedly living in a school that had an authorized enrolment of 225.[17]

In 1914, the Qu'Appelle school was discovered to have thirty-six "Halfbreed" students in attendance, even after they had discharged fifteen over the previous year. Indian Affairs threatened to cancel the grants if the children were not replaced with pupils who had status under the *Indian Act* by the next year.[18] One of the non-status children at the school was Louise Moine, who grew up in a Métis family in the Lac Pelletier Valley in Saskatchewan. By 1908, there were ten children in the family. It was her mother's decision to send the children to the Qu'Appelle residential school. Although the decision was not discussed at the time, in retrospect, Louise concluded her parents sent her and her siblings to residential school out of economic need and concern that their children receive a religious education. "There we would be housed, fed, clothed and educated at no cost whatever, except the train fare to and from the school. Also, it was a religious institution operated by priests and nuns, so my parents were assured that this part of our education would not be neglected."[19]

In her memoir, Moine wrote that she knew that she and other Métis children were not supposed to be at the school. She recalled that Indian Commissioner W. A. Graham was at the school on a regular basis. However, she wrote, if "Mr. Graham noticed any little strays around the place we never heard, so we remained."[20] In search of new students, Qu'Appelle principal Hugonnard travelled to the Assiniboine, Moose Mountain, Pipestone, and Oak Lake reserves with little success, reporting that he had "been able to replace only six half-breed pupils by Indian ones."[21] In writing about the St. Bernard school in Alberta in 1913, Bishop Grouard said that "to have a school at all it was necessary to board" both "Half breed and Indian children." The Métis children had not been numbered as Indians, and he had not collected grants for them from the government.[22]

By the end of 1913, Indian Affairs acknowledged that the 1910 contract amounted to a reversal of Sifton's policy, and announced that it would once more be admitting students with *Indian Act* status. Once more, "all children, even those of mixed blood, whether legitimate or not who live upon an Indian reserve and whose parents on either side live as Indians, even if they are not annuitants," would be eligible for admission to the schools. The policy change was accompanied by a warning from Duncan Campbell Scott:

> Abuses, however, must be guarded against and every application for admission
> should be accompanied by satisfactory evidence that the applicant is a halfbreed
> to whom the rule applies, and not a person who has been adopted by or
> otherwise brought into association with Indians with the express purpose of
> gaining admission to our schools.[23]

The impact of the federal school-admission rules, and their inconsistency, on Aboriginal family structure can be seen in the story of the family of Thomas Desjarlais, a Métis man originally from Manitoba. In the 1880s, he was living in Lebret, Saskatchewan, and had married a Métis woman from the Dakota Territory. His brother and sister were living as Treaty Indians on the nearby Muscowequan Reserve, while his wife's sister and husband were also Treaty Indians, living at the File Hills agency. Because Thomas Desjarlais and his wife wished to see their oldest daughter, Rosine, go to school, they arranged to have her adopted into her maternal aunt's family. On this basis, she was able to attend the Qu'Appelle school. There, according to family lore, she learned to speak several Aboriginal languages from other students, although, in later life, she downplayed her Aboriginal heritage and rarely spoke any of these languages.[24]

Those provincial governments that recognized an obligation to Métis children began buying space for them in residential schools. Starting in 1914, Alberta began sending orphans to the Roman Catholic school in Onion Lake, Saskatchewan.[25] Saskatchewan's deputy minister of education wrote to Indian Affairs in 1918, asking if it would be possible to have "white and half-breed" children educated at the residential school run by the Oblates at Lac la Plonge.[26] The Indian Affairs position was that they might be able to attend as day students, but could definitely not board at the school.[27]

By 1921, Indian Commissioner W. A. Graham concluded that "we are practically in the same position now as we were seven or eight years ago, by having our schools over-run by nontreaty Breeds." Graham also asked Ottawa, "Can non-Treaty parents take out their children from school and decide when to send them back?"[28] At the time, there were seventy-three Canadian residential schools in operation.[29] Indian Affairs was still called upon to adjudicate individual cases whereby children appeared to be both Métis and 'Indian' by way of parental transitions in and out of marriages, on and off reserves, and in other ways that changed family status under the *Indian Act*.

The experience of Métis Elder Mary Vitaline Flammand serves as another example of the barriers facing Métis people who sought to have their children attend school.[30] In 1922, her godfather and Cowessess band member Francis Delorme placed her in the Grayson, Saskatchewan, boarding school. She did not stay long: "I wasn't there for two weeks and I was thrown out."[31] Her father, Alexander Flammand, then attempted to enrol her, along with a younger sister, in a public school nearby at Dubuc. Because her family was living on road-allowance land and therefore not paying school taxes, she was removed from there on her first day. "So we came home and told our dad 'we can't go to school there, the government won't let us go to school there.' So then, he came back home and told my mother 'yeah that's right, the kids can't go to school there because we have to pay taxes.' So that was it, I never did go to school again."[32]

From the early 1920s until the 1940s, Métis parents faced numerous barriers if they wanted to provide their children with a formal education. Once again, the federal government had started to dismiss Métis students from residential schools, while the provinces, for cost reasons, were reluctant to ensure that they were admitted to public schools. In September 1925, Indian Affairs instructed the Beauval, Saskatchewan, school principal to discharge the forty-five "halfbreeds" at the school. According to the local Indian agent, Mr. Taylor, the school "could easily be filled" with Treaty children from the "Canoe Lake, Clear Lake, Portage la Loche and English River Bands."[33] Principal Lajeunesse responded that if Taylor were better acquainted with the "Chipewyan up north," he would not have said the school could be easily filled with their children. "We have tried every means (except by force) to have their children. The very few who did consent to send them would not allow them to come back after a year or two." He also pointed out that the school had never tried to hide the fact that the majority of its students were Métis. Furthermore, he said, only five of the forty-five students had living fathers and mothers. "You can imagine, the difficulty to find at once, where to place these destitute children."[34] The government dropped its demand for an immediate discharge of the Métis children, but expected that the majority of the students would be discharged by the end of June 1926.[35] Two years later, in December 1928, Indian Affairs secretary J. D. McLean wrote to the Beauval principal to request that he discharge the eight "half-breed" children on the school register.[36] The school defended their presence, referring to a November 19, 1922, memorandum from Indian Affairs Deputy Minister Duncan Campbell Scott, and stating, "There is a departmental ruling to the effect that half-breed children living the Indian mode of life on a reserve are eligible for admission to the boarding school."[37]

In 1927, the federal government gave the Oblate school at Brocket, Alberta, permission to admit female Métis students, on the condition that the band accept them as members after their graduation. Seven years later, when the principal repeated the request, he was informed that "absolutely no half-breed children can be admitted to our schools."[38]

In February 1928, three "half breed" children were admitted to the Onion Lake Anglican school after the death of their mother. This was done without the department's permission. In December 1929, Commissioner Graham reported that the Indian agent was still trying to have the children removed from the school, into the custody of either their father or the provincial Department of Neglected and Dependent Children.[39] Graham wrote that it had been "a hard struggle to keep halfbreeds out of our schools and if we are going to make exceptions and admit a few we are going to have a lot of trouble."[40] The following year, there were six Métis children attending the two residential schools in Onion Lake. Graham concluded that rather than remove the children, the Oblate provincial intended to let them remain there as long as Indian Affairs allowed them to stay.[41]

As the nation moved into a state of economic depression in the 1930s, Duncan Campbell Scott sent out instructions that children of questionable standing regarding their 'Indianness' should be discharged from schools "without delay," stressing the costs involved in maintaining these students in the school and reminding all involved that "the Indian Department is not conducting charitable institutions. There are provincial homes for cases of this kind, and principals of our schools must not take in children for sympathetic reasons."[42]

Persuading provincial governments to take responsibility for Métis children was proving to be a near-impossible task. In 1935, the Roman Catholic Bishop of Grouard pointed out to the Alberta minister of public works that for several years, Roman Catholic schools had been taking care of "quite a number of children (white and half-breed) that really were or should have been wards of the Government." At the time of writing, he said the church was taking care of at least 100 such children. Given that the provincial government had recently provided a grant to the Woods' Home in Calgary, he suggested that a similar grant might be made to the Catholic Church.[43]

In 1936, D. Robinson from Koostatak, Manitoba, wrote to Indian Affairs Minister T. A. Crerar, seeking permission to have his four children accepted into the Brandon residential school. Robinson wrote that his mother was a "member of the St. Peters Band of Indians my father was a non treaty Indian and I was adopted by John B. Stevenson who was treaty Indian of the St. Peters Band and my wife is still taking treaty as a member of the Peguis Band."

Because he was not an Indian under the *Indian Act*, his children had not been allowed admission to the school. But, he wrote, he was "unable to provide sufficient food or clothing for my children owing to the lack of work or anything to enable me to obtain necessary supplies." The principal of the Brandon school had informed him that there was room in the school for his children.[44] His appeal was denied because he was "not a Treaty Indian."[45]

The lack of education opportunities for Métis children on the Prairies led Métis political leader Malcolm Norris to observe:

> I have always understood that it was against the law not to send the children to school, and Inspectors are maintained for that very purpose, but unfortunately our people have been discriminated against, and to such an extent, that even though they may pay taxes, no steps are taken by the authorities to see that their children are sent to school, apparently the Half-breed is not worth caring about.[46]

It was this sort of frustration that led in the 1930s to the creation of l'Association des Métis d'Alberta et les Territoires du Nord-Ouest (also known as the "Metis Brotherhood of Alberta"), under the leadership of Joseph Dion (a teacher at Kehiwin), James Brady, Felix Callihoo, and Peter C. Tomkins, to represent "non-status Indians and Metis."[47] In response to its lobbying, the Alberta government appointed a Royal Commission in 1934 to study living conditions of Métis in the province.[48] James Brady made the principal Métis presentation to the commission, arguing for the establishment of self-governing Métis colonies. Education, he said, should be provided by Métis school boards on a non-denominational basis. His fear was that the government would establish government-administered colonies and schools, depriving the Métis of control of these central aspects of their lives.[49] Bishop Breynat challenged the Métis opposition to denominational education, telling the commissioners that "you cannot go by his advice anyway, that is the type of man who does not know—he is a very poor man."[50]

The commission's 1936 report observed that many people were of the "opinion that it is advantageous to take the half-breed child into a large boarding school and teach him the conveniences and amenities of modern life. The argument is that when he returns to his former life he will do so with a desire to approximate as nearly as circumstances will permit, the better life of his school days." Other presenters had told the commission that in such a circumstance, the student would be less able to meet the demands of life in a Métis community. In either case, it was obvious that where there was no white settlement, large numbers of children were growing up without any schooling.[51] Some evidence given to the commission suggested that "80 per cent of the half-breed children of the Province of Alberta receive no education whatever."[52] The commission recommended the establishment of Métis agricultural colonies under the supervision of government officials. In schools on the colonies, children could be taught "reading and writing and elementary arithmetic. In addition, the boys should be taught stock raising and farming, while the girls should be taught the elements of sanitation, cleanliness, sewing and knitting."[53] The report led to the adoption of the *Metis Population Betterment Act* in 1938. Under the Act, provincial land was set aside for Métis settlements.[54] As Métis leader James Brady had feared, the Alberta Bureau of Relief was given responsibility for services on the settlements, including education. Government-appointed officials administered the settlements.[55] Although the initial Act endorsed the value of "conferences and negotiations between" the provincial government and the Métis, this language was dropped from the Act in 1940.[56]

In 1937, Indian Affairs formally reversed Sifton's 1899 policy allowing the admission of Métis students to residential schools. In doing so, department secretary T. R. L. MacInnes wrote that the old policy had been adopted "at a time when the provincial governments and the government of the North West Territories were not in a position to provide educational facilities for the children of certain half-breed residents in the outlying sections of the Dominion." However, he stressed, "There has never been, nor is there now, any statutory obligation upon the Dominion Government to provide educational facilities for half-breed children." The federal government position was that the provincial governments—no mention was made of the territorial governments—were "now in a position to look after the education and welfare of these children."[57] Per capita grants would be made only "in the case of children of Indian paternal descent." Children enrolled in residential schools prior to September 1, 1937, would be exempt from the ruling.[58]

From 1889 to 1937, the federal government's admission policy for non-Indian students at residential schools had been far from consistent. There were two institutions during this period—the Île-à-la-Crosse school in northern Saskatchewan, and St. Paul's Hostel in Dawson City in the Yukon—that further demonstrate this lack of consistency. Both institutions received federal funding at various points in their history, even though most of the students who attended them were of mixed descent.

CHAPTER 4

Île-à-la-Crosse

Île-à-la-Crosse is the site of one of the oldest Roman Catholic missions in the Canadian West. The history of residential schooling at the mission is long and complex. In 1776, a Montréal-based trading company established a post at Île-à-la-Crosse in Saskatchewan.[1] The Hudson's Bay Company (HBC) also opened a post there in 1799.[2] After the 1821 merger of the HBC and the North West Company (NWC), Île-à-la-Crosse became the headquarters of the HBC's English River District brigade operations. In 1845, a Roman Catholic missionary visited the community.[3] The following year, Bishop Provencher sent two Oblates, Alexandre-Antonin Taché and Louis-François Lafleche, to establish a permanent mission at Île-à-la-Crosse.[4] They built the Saint-Jean-Baptiste mission on the site of the abandoned NWC post.[5]

By 1847, they were operating a day school for the children at the fort.[6] The Oblates were disappointed by the irregular attendance and sought the assistance of the Sisters of Charity in establishing a boarding school.[7] In 1860, three Sisters of Charity arrived at Île-à-la-Crosse and took ownership of the newly built Le Couvent Saint-Bruno.[8] According to Oblate officials, the majority of students at the school were Métis.[9]

In the mornings, both girls and boys were taught lessons in spoken and written French and in basic arithmetic. They also attended catechism class.[10] The lessons in the common room were preceded and followed by work routines. The girls were being prepared for service as homemakers, and worked daily in the school kitchen.[11] The boys did not sleep in the dormitory at the convent, but, instead, at the Oblate house, under the supervision of a lay brother.[12] At 5:30 a.m., he escorted them to Saint-Bruno, where they would work, eat, and receive lessons. They spent the afternoons on farm work.[13]

Reports from 1861 to 1863 indicate that the students made little headway in speaking, reading, or writing in French, the language of education at the school.[14] Instead, the children persisted in speaking Cree among themselves. The missionaries believed that the children's contact with Cree- and Chipewyan-speaking relatives was helping to keep language use alive. As a result, in 1861, they threatened to reduce the number of visits between families and students. However, this restriction was not implemented.[15]

The school was plagued by health problems and food shortages. In 1865, a student died of pleurisy (inflammation of the lining of the lungs). In the spring of 1866, the fishery failed completely, the school closed, and the children with relatives in the vicinity were sent home for two months.[16] In 1867, the boys' dormitory burned down.[17] A rebuilt dormitory opened in 1874.[18]

The Oblates successfully lobbied for federal funding in 1875.[19] However, the period of federal funding was short-lived. The grant was cut.[20] The rationale given was that Île-à-la-Crosse was outside the limits of Treaty 6.[21] In the years following, little or no funding was provided.[22]

Parents at Île-à-la-Crosse continued to object to the treatment their children received at the school. Deaths of children, such as that of a four-year-old in 1875, led some local families to accuse the Oblates and Sisters of Charity of either negligence or being too harsh in disciplining the children.[23] In a letter to her brother Louis, Sara Riel complained of the parents' lack of gratitude, writing, "Here in the North our people, the Métis, do not appreciate the benefits of instruction.... We are required to fight against the indifference and caprice of children as well as against the weaknesses of their parents." For example, she was unable to convince the parents that English lessons benefited the students. In the face of persistent protest, the lessons were dropped in 1876.[24] Illness was also common; Sara Riel, herself, died of tuberculosis in 1883.[25] In that year, there were only twenty-seven students on the roll, with an average daily attendance of twenty-three.[26] Following the 1885 North-West Rebellion, the school was down to six residents: all orphans.[27]

During the early years of the twentieth century, the school was relocated to Lac la Plonge.[28] In 1917, the Sisters of Charity returned to Île-à-la-Crosse, where a new convent, the School of the Holy Family, had been constructed on higher ground. The dormitory housed four boarders, and classes were attended by twenty-two day students.[29] The school continued to be accompanied by disaster. Fire destroyed the convent on April 1, 1920. A replacement building, completed in October 1921, burned in 1925.[30] Three boys and one of the teaching sisters drowned in a boating accident in September 1923.[31]

Thérèse Arcand attended the school in the 1920s. She said that the day started between 5:30 and 6:00 in the morning. "We'd have to carry our own water. We washed up and made our beds before we came down and said our morning prayers."[32] That was followed by a breakfast of porridge that the students had prepared. Girls were assigned the task of washing the dishes. Children had other chores as well: there was milk to separate, clothing to mend, and the garden to tend. "We didn't play in the morning. This was work time."[33]

Classes began at 9:00 a.m. According to Arcand, "We didn't have scribblers in those days, we had slates. We had a little cloth to wipe them clean." Morning lessons were taught in French and included French grammar, spelling, reading, and arithmetic.

Before dinner, the pupils studied Bible history. Dinner at noon was a rushed affair: "we always hurried our eating—I don't think I even bothered to chew my food—[because] it was play time. It was a great penance if some of us had to be assigned to do the dishes. Playing was done outside."[34] Afternoon lessons were taught in English, and included geography; history; and English reading, spelling, and grammar. At 3:30, before the students left the school, they sang for fifteen minutes. Then, they were allowed half an hour of outdoor play. From 4:30 to 5:00 p.m., there was sewing, followed by prayer. The children attended supper, engaged in a final round of chores, and were sent to prepare for bed at 7:30. Lights were out at 8:00 p.m.[35]

By 1929, the number of boarders had increased to forty-two and the provincial government provided grants for the Métis day students who were attending the school.[36] The school may have closed several times before reopening in 1935.[37]

After the 1944 Saskatchewan election, the newly elected Co-operative Commonwealth Federation government commissioned a report on the state of education in northern Saskatchewan. At that time, less than half of the school-aged children in the region were attending school. There were only two public schools in the entire region, the rest being a mixture of largely unregulated, church-run schools. The government report called for the opening of more day schools and two large residential schools, one in the eastern part of the province and one in the western part, which would be operated without church involvement. The school on the western side of the province was to be located in Île-à-la-Crosse. But neither provincially operated residential school was established, in large measure due to lack of support from the federal government and opposition from the Catholic Church. Blocked by lack of federal support, the Saskatchewan government agreed to rent classrooms from the mission school, pay the mission schoolteachers' salaries, and help pay for the students' board.[38]

A larger building was opened in 1946. By 1947, there were 168 registered students being taught in five classrooms; 124 of these students were boarders.[39] By 1959, another new school had been built to accommodate 231 students. Of these, 113 were boarders. In 1964, the boys' boarding house burned down.[40] At the time of the fire, there were 331 students at the school; about 100 were being boarded.[41] In 1972, the school caught fire again. Twelve classrooms were completely destroyed. At the same time, local parents were demanding greater control over education in the community. As a result, the Île-à-la-Crosse boarding school was closed and replaced by the locally administered Rossignol elementary and Rossignol high schools.[42] Métis architect Douglas Cardinal was commissioned to design the elementary school building.[43]

Two Métis children with an Inuit child at an Anglican residential school in northern Canada.

Library and Archives Canada, J. F. Moran, Department of Indian Affairs and Northern Development fonds, PA-102086.

In his 1879 report for the federal government, titled Report on Industrial Schools for Indians and Half-Breeds, Nicholas Flood Davin had proposed a central role in residential schooling and in assimilation in general for people of mixed descent, proclaiming them the "natural mediator between the Government and the red man, and also his natural instructor."
Saskatchewan Archives Board, R-A6665.

Louis Riel, the Métis founder of Manitoba and leader of the North-West Rebellion of 1885, taught at a boarding school for Métis boys in Montana in the 1880s. His sister, Sara Riel, worked at the Île-à-la-Crosse, Saskatchewan, school.
Glenbow Museum, NA-504-3.

Girls at the Île-à-la-Crosse, Saskatchewan, school in the early twentieth century.
Museum, Thomas Waterworth, PD-353-22.

The Saint-Paul-des-Métis, Alberta, school was built on a colony for Métis people that the Oblate order established in 1896 in what is now Alberta. The school was destroyed by a fire set by students in 1905.

Dechâtelets Archives, Oblates of Mary Immaculate collection.

In 1900, only fourteen of thirty-four students at the Anglican school in Onion Lake, Saskatchewan, had Treaty status. Many of the remaining twenty students were likely to have been Métis.

General Synod Archives, Anglican Church of Canada, P7538-339.

The Calgary Indian Industrial School football team in 1905. James Gladstone is in the middle of the middle row.
Glenbow Museum, NA-3-1.

THE BOYS and MR JORLIN I.I.S. Red Deer

In 1909, seventeen of the forty-five students at the Red Deer, Alberta, school were Métis.
United Church of Canada Archives, 93 049P849N.

In 1914, the Qu'Appelle school was discovered to have thirty-six "half-breed" students in attendance, even after the school had discharged fifteen over the previous year. Indian Affairs threatened to cancel the grants if the children were not replaced by the next year with pupils who had status under the Indian Act.

Library and Archives Canada, Mines and Technical Surveys, PA-023092.

Bishop Isaac Stringer and Métis students at the Dawson City hostel.

Yukon Archives, 82-332, #28.

Sister McQuillan and students at the Fort Resolution school in the Northwest Territories. In 1922, Roman Catholic Bishop Gabriel Breynat arranged to have the federal government pay for the upkeep of eight Métis students enrolled in the school.
Henry Jones. Hudson's Bay Company Archives, Provincial Archives of Manitoba, 1987, 363-I-47.1/1 (N60-2).

Métis students at the Anglican hostel in Whitehorse in the Yukon Territories. In 1955, there were thirty-one students living in the hostel.
General Synod Archives, Anglican Church of Canada, P7561-219.

The Sturgeon Lake school was one of the Alberta residential schools with a high enrolment of Métis students.
Dechâtelets Archives, Oblates of Mary Immaculate collection; Provincial Archives of Alberta, J. L. Irwin, A6978.

Rita Evans went to the Grouard, Alberta, school for four years. Religious instruction and drudge work, with very little emphasis on classroom education, loom large in her memory of the school.
Dechâtelets Archives, Oblates of Mary Immaculate collection.

The Joussard, Alberta, school enrolled a large number of Métis students in the 1950s.
Dechâtelets Archives, Oblates of Mary Immaculate collection.

In 1951, R. S. Davis, the regional director of Indian agencies in Manitoba, recommended that the principal of the Sandy Bay, Manitoba, school be instructed to expel three "half-breeds" from the school.
Saint Boniface Historical Society, Oblates of Mary Immaculate, Manitoba Province fonds, SHSB22623

CHAPTER 5

Métis residential school education in the North

The Yukon hostels

Many of the early Roman Catholic mission schools had been established to provide educational opportunities for the children of European fur-trade employees and their Aboriginal wives. Once northern Treaties were signed, people of mixed descent were often encouraged by Roman Catholic clergy to take Treaty, in large measure to ensure that their children would be accepted into residential schools. After the creation of the provinces of Alberta and Saskatchewan in 1905, the Northwest and Yukon territories were truly northern territories—large in area but with a comparatively small population. In the first half of the twentieth century, neither territory had a well-developed public school system. For most of that period, the churches operated the only schools in the Northwest Territories (NWT).[1] In the Yukon, the government presence in the region shrank with each decade. By the early 1930s, one man, George Jeckell, served as the region's financial controller, tax inspector, land titles registrar, public works agent, and chief executive officer—and mayor of Dawson City. Here, as in the NWT, such education that existed was provided by the churches.[2]

In the Yukon, the Anglican Church made an initial attempt to provide residential schooling to Aboriginal children in the late nineteenth century, when Bishop William Bompas took children into the Forty Mile Mission. In 1894, he had six students: four of mixed ancestry, and two First Nations children. Bompas had trouble getting funding for the school from the Church Missionary Society, which objected to his desire to focus on educating children of mixed descent. He felt that such children, if educated, could become the church's best advocates, but would otherwise follow the cultural practices of their mothers, who were often First Nations women.[3] Bompas transferred the school to Carcross in 1903, where it eventually became the Chooutla school. When that school began receiving federal support as a residential school, there was an expectation that it would not accept Métis students. Bompas's successor, Isaac Stringer, sought to have a separate home for children of Métis families, where the students might be able to share the Carcross school's facilities. The plan was abandoned for lack of federal support.[4]

In 1919, W. W. Williams of the Anglican Church recommended that the church establish a facility for non-status children in Dawson City. Citing a particular family whose children had lost their mother and needed more care than their father could provide, Williams argued for the development of a boarding facility to house students who would attend local schools. He was convinced that a "good Motherly woman to take care of the children could be found among the church people." Unless the church took action, Williams wrote to his bishop, "there is nowhere but the fold of the R.C. church for such children and the R.C.s make the most of the situation."[5]

The Anglican Forward Movement, an Anglican missionary fund, provided the money to purchase a house in Dawson City to be used as a residence for students from Métis families from remote communities. Miss E. J. Naftel, who had been working at the school in Carcross, was appointed superintendent. Known as "St. Paul's," the hostel opened in 1920.[6] By 1922, a log extension had been added to the hostel, allowing it to accommodate nineteen children. In that year, Stringer requested $4,000 in federal support. He ended his letter of request with a reminder: "By means of this Institution many children will be given a chance to become good and useful citizens instead of a menace to the country."[7]

In 1922, the federal government agreed to provide the hostel with financial support. Although Indian Affairs provided the funding, it took the position that it was not assuming responsibility for the hostel on the "same basis as the Indian Residential Schools." It was "acting simply as the agent of the Department of the Interior."[8] A 1923 Privy Council document, however, described the school as being conducted "for the benefit of destitute and orphan half-breeds and forms part of the educational system of the Department of Indian Affairs."[9] In the summer of 1923, the Anglicans purchased a former Good Samaritan hospital building for use as a dormitory.[10] Within two years of the hostel's founding, there had been a complete change in staff. The former head of the Carcross school, C. F. Johnson, and his wife took over the running of the hostel.[11]

In 1924, an outbreak of measles led to the hostel's being placed in quarantine. Some of the residents of Dawson City placed responsibility for the outbreak on Bishop Stringer, who, they felt, had brought measles to the community by recruiting infected students. There was talk of banning the residence's students from the public schools, but this did not happen.[12] For the three months the quarantine was in place, the principal's wife taught lessons to the children.[13]

Principal Johnson sought to exercise control over the students' out-of-class behaviour. In the spring of 1927, alarmed by the amount of time that one young woman, who was boarding at the hostel while working for a family in the community, was spending with a local man, Johnson "had the man up before Major Allard" of the local police detachment. Johnson said that after he gave the girl "a talking to," her father withdrew her from the residence. The following year, she returned to the residence and continued to work at a private home.[14] The older children, sometimes close to eighteen years old, often had objections to schooling. Johnson could sympathize with one of them, saying, "She is a grown woman weighing in the neighbourhood of 160 lbs and then having to associate with the children in the primary grades."[15]

By 1939, the Dawson hostel, which was being run by a Mrs. McLain, required parents to sign an agreement that they would not withdraw their children from the hostel until they were grown. The hostel had introduced this policy because, in the past, parents had removed their children, "with the result that all the care in respect to the child has been rendered valueless by the subsequent care of the child by the parents themselves."[16]

The per capita funding that had been established for the hostel in 1923 was $250. It remained unchanged for the next twenty years. But, in 1943, Indian Affairs education official R. A. Hoey recommended that the payment be shifted from Indian Affairs to "the Branch responsible for the education and welfare of the population of the Yukon other than Indians."[17] The Indian Affairs position was that if it continued to fund the hostel, it would be obliged to fund Métis students living in residential schools. The Department of Mines and Resources—which had taken over responsibility for northern issues from the Department of the Interior—sought to have the Yukon territorial government take responsibility for the hostel.[18] Although the Yukon council initially rejected providing funding to a church-run institution, it eventually agreed to take over funding for twenty-two "indigent half-breed and white children" at the school, while noting that this move should not be seen as a precedent.[19]

The residents were kept busy. According to a report from 1949, the girls began to learn to iron clothing "at eight when they iron hankies, then pillowcase and aprons, and by the time they are fifteen they are able to do the boys [sic] dress shirts and school dresses very nicely. Each child is expected to iron ten–twelve articles each week." The boys were "kept busy in the wood-yard, splitting, packing, etc. and shoveling snow." During the summer, the children also went to church camp.[20]

In 1952, the principal noted that one of the major tasks at the school was making sure the furnace was constantly fed during the winter. The handyman stayed up all night, and the principal and the cook, with some help from the boys, stoked the fire during the day. The principal and the handyman took care of the garden, since most of the boys were small and the "work is beyond their strength and skill." Much of the moose meat and salmon that were fed to the students was purchased from local Aboriginal people.[21]

Throughout the 1930s, enrolment varied between seventeen and thirty students, but in the 1940s, it ranged between twenty-eight and forty-three.[22] By 1950, enrolment was being affected by two trends. A public school had been opened in Old Crow, so children from that community no longer needed to be boarded at the Dawson hostel. At the same time, the Yukon government started boarding Métis and white students at federal residential schools. As a result, the St. Paul's school was running a deficit.[23]

The hostel continued to operate until the fall of 1953, when the remaining few children were relocated to a church-run building in Carcross to attend the local public school.[24] Throughout the hostel's history, the majority of children in residence had been of mixed ancestry. In 1952, the principal wrote that of the students at the hostel, "all are partly Indian."[25]

In the early 1950s, the Anglican Church opened the St. Agnes hostel in Whitehorse for non-Aboriginal and mixed-ancestry students.[26] Originally located in an army hut, it was renovated in 1953. The building could house approximately thirty children in "cubicles of four to six beds."[27] In 1955, there were thirty-one students living in the hostel.[28] The residence also housed First Nations children who were attending high school in Whitehorse.[29] Clara Tizya, an Aboriginal woman who had worked at the Carcross school for thirteen years, went to work at the Yukon hostel in 1961 and became matron of St. Agnes in 1965.[30] The hostel closed in 1966.[31]

Métis residential education in the Northwest Territories

While the Anglicans were the dominant force in residential schooling in the Yukon, the Roman Catholic Church prevailed in the Northwest Territories. In the early 1920s, as Bishop Stringer was seeking support for a hostel in Dawson City, Gabriel Breynat, the Roman Catholic Bishop of Mackenzie, was lobbying for support for the education of non-status children at Fort Providence and Fort Resolution. Many of the parents of these children, he wrote, "are living like Indians, and should be included in the Treaty." The only grant the church received for these children was $400 a year for a day school. Such schools, he said, "have proved a failure in the North, as many of those half-breeds spend several months in the year in the bush, hunting for a living, thus in order to have an education, the children must remain as Boarders."[32]

Indian Affairs was not prepared to fund the education of non-status Aboriginal children in the Northwest Territories. Duncan Campbell Scott's 1921 comments on the issue were definitive: "We have no funds provided for the education of half-breed children."[33] The Northwest Territories Branch, the federal agency responsible for the territories, was equally unsupportive. The branch's first director, O. S. Finnie, recommended against accommodating Breynat's request, saying that most Métis had been offered the choice of taking Treaty or scrip. In his opinion, the government was not obligated to pay for the education of those who chose to take scrip, many of whom, he wrote, "have substantial revenues from their labor and trapping and can well afford to pay for the education of their children. If the Department subsidizes one sectarial [sic] school, it might be necessary to subsidize others."[34]

The Inuit and Métis children who were enrolled in the residential schools in the Northwest Territories did not receive the same benefits as other students. For example, in 1913, they were not given the same supplies that were provided to First Nations students who were leaving the schools: a rifle, ammunition, traps, and twine for the boys; and sewing kits for the girls.[35]

In 1922, Breynat succeeded in having eight Métis children designated as destitute and sending them to Fort Resolution. He asked the territorial government to pay $165 per student (the same amount being paid for Indian children). The policy that was developed was to pay $145 for children seven to fifteen years of age. For children younger than that, the government would pay $80 per year. It became policy not to admit Métis students unless they were destitute.[36] However, three years later, the federal government agreed to support "half-breeds who are living the Indian mode of life with Indian communities."[37]

In 1929, Breynat wrote to Finnie, saying that it had "become quite impossible" to support children on the "$145 per annum, for destitute half-breeds," and requesting the amount be increased to $180, "the amount allowed for Indians."[38] The fees were increased in keeping with Breynat's request.[39] In 1933, the three Roman Catholic schools (Fort Resolution, Fort Providence, and Aklavik) and two Anglican schools (Hay River and Shingle Point) were housing thirty-seven female and forty male "destitute children" in addition to the First Nations children. Fifty-four of these seventy-seven children were at Aklavik and Shingle Point. It was decided in that year that the female students would be kept in the schools until they reached the age of eighteen. Until that point, they had been discharged at the age of sixteen.[40]

The federal government was concerned about the number of destitute children it was supporting, and demanded annual reports on the families' ability to pay. When it was discovered that the widowed father of two children had remarried, the department conducted a detailed investigation into his earnings. The Mounted Police thought the man should be able to support the two children who were in residential school, although the Indian agent pointed out that this would leave him with nothing to support the two children that his new wife had brought into the family. In another case, the trapping records of a man described as a "cripple" were reviewed to see if he could be forced to pay for his children's schooling. In both cases, it was decided to continue to support the children in residential school.[41]

Racial attitudes were long-lived. In a 1935 assessment of which non-Indian students attending residential schools in the Northwest Territories should be provided with support, Assistant Deputy Minister of the Interior R. A. Gibson wrote of a thirteen-year-old boy attending the Shingle Point school: "In view of his partial white blood it is probable that he would benefit more from schooling than a full-blooded Eskimo and therefore should be kept in school until he reaches the maximum age of fourteen years."[42]

Enforcing attendance was also a problem. In 1941, Bishop Breynat asked Ottawa to implement compulsory attendance for "whites and especially for the half-breeds" in the territories, saying "half-breed" parents did not understand their duty to "provide a sound intellectual and moral training" for their children."[43] It was pointed out to him that the Territorial Schools Ordinance required parents of children between seven and twelve years of age to send their child to "school for a period of at least sixteen weeks in each year at least eight weeks of which time shall be consecutive."[44] In order to help them gain access to schools, into the 1940s, the Catholic Church campaigned to have northern Métis admitted to Treaty. Between 1930 and 1943, for example, 164 people were admitted to Treaty in the NWT.[45]

As late as 1944, Anglican Bishop A. L. Fleming was expressing concern about the territorial government's continued unwillingness to provide educational services to Métis children. He wrote, "Unless the government is prepared to meet the situation we are bound to be involved in the old trouble of an illiterate half-breed population, ineffective and ofttimes undesirable."[46]

In the mid-1950s, the federal government finally took responsibility for education in the North. This led to the closing of most of the mission schools and the establishment of a series of hostels and day schools. These hostels and schools did not restrict admission to children with status under the *Indian Act*, but were open to all children in the Northwest Territories and the Yukon. This development both increased the educational opportunities available to Métis children and increased the number of Métis children living away from their parents in residential conditions. The history of these hostels and schools is discussed in a separate part of the report on the history of residential schools.

CHAPTER 6

Provincial responsibility: 1940–1960

The 1937 policy change was a clear indication that the federal government expected the provinces to take over responsibility for Métis education, whether in a residential or non-residential setting. This was in keeping with the overall approach that the federal government took towards First Nations education in the years following World War Two, which was to integrate students into the provincial system. In the case of First Nations students, the federal government recognized a financial responsibility to pay the provinces to educate First Nations students. It did not accept a similar responsibility for Métis education. Since, in many parts of western and northern Canada, Métis students lived in communities where there were no day schools, provincial governments often chose to place them in residential schools. In some cases, spaces were purchased in federally supported residential schools, while, in other cases, the spaces were in schools operated solely by religious organizations. Over time, provincial governments established northern school divisions. Although these divisions opened elementary schools in many small and remote communities, high school education often was provided in central locations only, with students being required to live in residences. As a result, many Métis students continued to receive residential schooling—often in federally funded institutions—well into the post-war period. A similar process in the Yukon and Northwest Territories expanded Métis attendance in northern residential schools.

It is important to recognize that Métis children and parents often were not welcomed into public schools. Saskatchewan Superintendent of Schools J. R. Martin wrote in 1941 that Métis children in one community had such severe health problems that if the government forced them to attend school, "the other children would walk out and refuse to go to school."[1] In 1943, Martin's successor, E. J. Brandt, reported, "Some parents even threaten to take their children out of school if more of the Métis attend. On the surface this seems to be a very narrow and bigoted attitude but if we examine the matter more closely from the point of view of health and cleanliness, they may be, at least partly justified."[2] Public opinion was scandalized in Saskatchewan after the 1942 trial of a thirteen-year-old Métis boy for his theft of a horse and buggy. The trial detailed the plight of the Métis families of the Crescent Lake region of the province. During the winter, they lived in shacks, and travelled during the summer. The investigation revealed there were at least forty school-aged children in the community who had never gone to school. These children were described in a police report as being malnourished and suffering from a number of diseases, including tuberculosis and trachoma, which was a potential cause of blindness.[3] Such stories generated public sympathy towards the Métis while, at the same time, reinforcing resistance to the prospect of the enrolment of Métis children in public schools.

Initially, the federal government seems to have opposed efforts to continue the policy of placing Métis children in residential schools. In January 1940, Indian agent N. P. L'Heureux, who was responding to an overcrowding problem at the Fort Vermilion school, informed the school principal, J. Huguerre, that it "is useless to present to Ottawa, an application for the admission" of an eight-year-old girl, whose parents were both "non-treaty." L'Heureux said he would not recommend admission because "there are still many Indian children who are treaty and who are not in school."[4] At the time, there were eighty-eight students enrolled in a school with a designated capacity of sixty-five.[5] The overcrowding problem was largely one of the government's own creation. Earlier that month, Dr. H. A. Hamman had informed Indian Affairs that

> more and more children are being brought into the (Fort Vermillion Residential) school in accordance with your instructions that various adults will lose ration rights if their children or grandchildren are not placed therein. Accommodation is taxed to the utter limit and more are coming. Not a single cot is now available. But, more important, the health of all is going to be seriously affected if more are entered as the cubic air space of dormitories and school rooms is already asked to do too much to keep up a steady amount of fresh air for all.[6]

Also in 1940, Indian agent Samuel Lovell reported that Father Doyen, the principal of the Guy Hill school in The Pas, Manitoba, was "in the habit of taking destitute half-breed children into the School as resident pupils." Lovell pointed out that this was done without any medical examination.[7] Indian Affairs official Philip Phelan informed Lovell that it was against policy to admit "destitute halfbreed children to the Guy Indian Residential School." If any such children had been admitted, Lovell was expected to instruct the principal to discharge them. The maintenance of "destitute halfbreed children" was deemed a provincial responsibility.[8]

In Manitoba, federal opposition to Métis enrolment in residential schools continued through the 1940s and early 1950s. In 1946, Indian Affairs declined to admit four children to the Birtle, Manitoba, school as grant-earning students, because their father was a "French Halfbreed."[9] In 1951, R. S. Davis, the regional director of Indian agencies in Manitoba, recommended that the principal of the Sandy Bay, Manitoba, school be instructed to return three "half breeds" to their homes and have their places taken by "Treaty Indians." Davis noted that he was led to believe that Indian Affairs was currently paying for the three students' education.[10]

The trend was very different in Alberta where there were six church-owned residential schools in operation. These schools did not require government approval to admit students who did not have status under the *Indian Act*.[11] As result, the Roman Catholic schools at Hobbema, Fort Vermilion, Grouard, Fort Chipewyan, Joussard, and Wabasca began to take in increasing numbers of Métis students in the 1940s and 1950s.

By 1946, the Alberta Department of Education was paying the Roman Catholic Diocese of Grouard $500 a year for every group of thirty-five provincial students it accepted. Almost all of them would be Métis. In that year, the department supported ninety-seven students.[12] The number of Métis students attending the Catholic Sturgeon Lake school was so great that, according to Bishop Henri Routhier, they presented a problem in terms of "hygiene and discipline," and were contributing to what he described as "unduly overcrowde[d]" classrooms.[13]

Provincial support for Métis students in residential schools was haphazard. In 1950, the Alberta government was paying $900 a year to support Métis students at the Holy Angels school in Fort Chipewyan. According to G. H. Gooderham, the regional supervisor of Indian agencies in Alberta, "There are a great many Metis attending the Residential School at Grouard," but the "Province has paid nothing for their tuition."[14] According to Bishop Routhier, in the summer of 1950, the province was paying $18 a month to cover board, tuition, and clothing of Métis students at Roman Catholic boarding schools. In a letter to the Alberta government, Routhier noted that Indian Affairs was paying "a little over $300 a year per child," or $25 a month, and suggested that the province should pay a similar amount.[15]

By 1951, one inspector thought that the Grouard school was developing into "an orphanage for metis and white children." The First Nations population was down to one-third of the school and was expected to drop further when First Nation students from the Yukon transferred to the recently constructed Lower Post school on the British Columbia–Yukon border. One possibility was to transfer the First Nations students at Grouard to Joussard, and turn Grouard over to the provincial government, to be used as a Métis school. An inspector noted that "the thin stream of school supplies fed by the Indian Affairs Branch is thinly spread with a meagre reinforcement from provincial or other funds for the five classrooms." According to the inspector, "the smooth running and efficient operation of the school is achieved at the expense of the childrens' [sic] education. Self-expression and self-confidence are sacrificed to regimentation and efficiency."[16] In October that year, Indian Affairs official Philip Phelan noted that only 50 of the 175 students at Grouard had status under the *Indian Act*. He suggested that they be placed in other schools. "This would mean that all the Metis children would be in the same building. It would also mean that the other schools would only have Indian children."[17] The church was able to deflect this proposal. In 1954, there were sixty-four Indian children attending the school, and Bishop Routhier took the position that he would prefer to see the school continue to educate both "Indian children and ... Metis children."[18] This trend continued elsewhere. In 1958, there were twenty-seven (twenty-five after Christmas) Métis children attending the Wabasca school.[19] In December 1958, only 7 of the 250 students at the mission school at Grouard were Treaty students; almost all the rest were Métis.[20]

In 1960, the Alberta government established the Northlands School Division to coordinate education throughout northern Alberta. The division incorporated thirty school districts and twenty schools.[21] In coming years, other districts would transfer into the division.[22] In 1961, the province purchased the Grouard hostel with the intent to convert it into a residence for students attending a vocational training centre, to be built in the community. This was the largest residential project operated by Northlands. It opened in 1963, but was closed several years later, due to costs and low enrolment. An ongoing problem for the school was the fact that Aboriginal students did not feel accepted in the local public schools.[23]

The Saskatchewan government attempted to reform its northern education in the 1940s, but it was not until the 1970s that the residential school in Île-à-la-Crosse closed and was replaced by a public school.[24] In Manitoba, the Frontier School Division was established in 1965.[25] A former military base at Cranberry Portage was converted into a residence for students from remote communities attending high school.

It is apparent that many of the past issues associated with residential schooling of Métis children have continued into the present. A 2010 review of Alberta's Northlands School Division found that the division's students had low rates of high school completion. Furthermore, many students who did go on to high school still had to leave the division and board in larger communities, where very few supports were available to them. Whether they were bused to, or boarded at, outside schools, many students felt that the reception they received in public schools was racist. In addition, the Aboriginal content provided in the division's schools was judged to be "inadequate."[26] Based on the evidence of the students who attended residential schools, it is clear that the education Métis people experienced in the residential school system paralleled that of First Nations and Inuit students.

CHAPTER 7

The students speak

Métis students and students of mixed descent were present in the residential school system throughout its history. In some cases, they were forced to attend. In other cases, these were the only schools open to them. Their parents often made tremendous financial sacrifices to ensure that their children went to these schools. Once Métis children were enrolled, their residential school experiences were characterized by

- a sharp and often tragic break from their family;
- a bewildering immersion in a foreign and highly regimented culture;
- harsh discipline;
- vulnerability to abuse;
- an educational regime that placed more focus on religion and work than on academics; and
- a limited, monotonous, and unappealing diet.

Despite this, not all Métis students give negative accounts of their school years. Some recall kind teachers, and are grateful for the skills that they acquired. For others, the only positive memories are of the friendships and alliances they formed in response to what they perceived as harsh and sometimes abusive discipline and mistreatment at the hands of school bullies.

Métis children might have gone to residential schools for a wide variety of reasons. In some cases, it might be due to the death of a parent. Angie Crerar, who attended the Fort Resolution school for ten years, recalled her childhood as being happy and secure, surrounded by three sisters, four brothers, and two loving parents. "My mother did a lot of gardening, and she did a lot of herbal medicine. My dad worked at the Hudson's Bay Company and also as an interpreter." She said that her father "instilled in us the value and the pride of being Métis." In 1948, her mother became ill with tuberculosis, and Crerar and two of her siblings were sent to residential school. Her mother died two days after she got there. "We only heard about it a week later. A nun took us into a room and told us: 'You are now orphans. Your mother is dead.' I remember holding my sisters. I remember crying. I remember feeling so alone and so lost and so very lonely."[1]

Theresa Meltenberger went to the Lac La Biche school in Alberta for five years while her parents spent much of their time, according to her, "in the bush." Her mother placed her in school because "education was her main priority."[2]

Elmer Cardinal went to the Catholic school in St. Albert, Alberta, for eight years, leaving when he turned sixteen. He felt that the most positive part of his life was his early childhood when he was raised by his grandparents. That ended when the local priest and the Indian agent arranged for him to be sent to school.[3]

For most students, the first days at school were very hard. Alphonse Janvier, who spent five years at the Île-à-la-Crosse school in Saskatchewan, described being separated from his parents as "the hardest experience in my life." He has never forgotten the feeling of being "a seven or eight year old child put on a red plane—taxiing away from your mom standing on shore, crying. It seems like a long time ago, but it's also very fresh in my memory, and that was my very first experience of the feeling of abandonment." Neither has he forgotten the anger and hurt he felt on arrival. "I was put on this old barber's chair. I remember my head being shaved and all my long hair falling on the floor, and the way they dealt with my crying and the hurtful feeling was with a bowl of ice cream."[4] Robert Derocher, who called the time he spent at Île-à-la-Crosse "the worst year that I ever lived," recalled being punished for speaking Cree. "It was so hard, you know, not to be able to communicate with other native children there."[5] Theresa Meltenberger travelled to the school first by train, and then by sleigh in the company of an Oblate brother. "It was my first time away from home and this was all very traumatic in a way."[6]

Even Thérèse Arcand, who reported being "happy" at Île-à-la-Crosse, and went on to become a Grey Nun herself, observed that "at the same time, I was very, very lonesome. I should have come to school the year before, I guess, but, I couldn't decide to leave my mother."[7] She described returning to school after holidays as emotionally wrenching: "We stayed there the best part of two months. At the middle of August we had to come back to school again, and, I just cried! I never found it easy to leave home. Never! I went home for the summers of '22 and '23 and then I didn't go back home again."[8]

One former Métis student's story provides a vivid account of arrival at a residential school in Alberta in the mid-twentieth century.

> The first day that I arrived at the residential school, my brother was comforting me as was my father and mother. I think at that time, I was more mad than I was sad to see them go because they didn't tell me I was gonna be staying at the mission when they went home. I remember my brother was standing beside me trying to comfort me because I was crying and then very soon afterwards they called us inside for supper. We were served our food and we were assigned to a

table. I really didn't know what to do so I got up and talked to my older brother. I asked him what to do and he kinda whispered to me to feed myself. Before I reached my table, the nun was screaming at me. I didn't know what she said, but I knew the tone and it wasn't nice. I broke her rules. I got up from my place and I was talking Cree.[9]

James Thomas spent ten years at the Grouard school in Alberta. His mother had died when he was about four. During his time at the school, he worked in the power shop, the blacksmith shop, and the vegetable fields. His family did not have enough money to bring him home during the holidays. In fact, Thomas believed that it took all of his father's modest earnings to "keep us down there."[10]

Martha Mercredi went into the Holy Angels convent at Fort Chipewyan, Alberta, when she was orphaned at the age of four. She stayed there for eight years. "I was treated very well. I didn't talk the language that I was supposed to talk (Cree), but I learned it from a friend when I was in the convent. We'd talk Cree because the nuns didn't understand Cree, we were being naughty, but the Sisters never knew that we were talking about them." She came to view the nuns as her family. "Sister Superior was my grandmother and the Sister Lucy was the teacher and she was like my momma, she's the one that's my guardian. So I have no complaint about the convent. I am very glad that they showed me how to read and write."[11]

Many students recalled the food as being inadequate, poorly prepared, and lacking in variety. Magee Shaw said, "The boys used to come across the road with the fish in big black buckets. It looked like they weren't scaled or anything—they were just black, big black pans. Breakfast was porridge, no milk, no sugar and you were always sitting in silence in a big room."[12] One Métis woman who attended an Alberta school recalled being fed "the same thing everyday, we never had toast, a girl used to come out with crusts of toast from the priest and the nuns and the kids would be all out there fighting for them or even orange peelings. We were hungry all the time. It seemed like the food was really greasy, soup with vegetables in it and we had to eat everything." Children who had been judged to be well behaved might be called up for seconds. But even they would go into the garden to "swipe carrots and tomatoes and stuff and try and hide them. If we got caught we would get a good strap."[13] The only time there was an improvement in the food, one student recalled, was if there was a visit from an outsider. "They used to put table cloths [sic] on the table and give us bacon and eggs to make it look like it was really good food, you know."[14] Another Métis student recalled that "every time the Bishop visited the mission, the food was better. It could have included pork chops or chicken or something better than what was the usual fare. The only other time that happened was when the Inspector of Indian Affairs came and also on those occasions you were given better clothing to wear."[15]

Another student said,

> At times we went hungry, it was always the same food, mush in the morning
> no sugar. They would just put a little bit on top to sprinkle it—the big boys got a
> little bit of milk, a little bit of brown sugar—three or four of the bigger boys they
> were the ones that got it. You could eat all the bread you want but you got one
> teaspoon of lard.

Because they always had beans at dinner, the students came to be known as "mission beans."[16]

Rita Evans went to the Grouard school for four years. Religious instruction and drudge work, with very little emphasis on classroom education, loom large in her memory of the school. "We were forever praying and not learning anything and when I came out of grade six, my goodness, I didn't know nothing you know except work, work. Very few made it to grade eight."[17] Church service often seemed like torture, particularly to the younger students. Of her time at the Grouard school, Evans said, "I'm not saying there's anything wrong with the church. I still go every chance I get, but we were tiny little kids. We're crying, why didn't they just leave them in bed with one girl looking after them? They don't know what mass is and that was just horrible."[18]

Life in the schools could quickly turn tragic. Colin Courtoreille told of how rapidly one boy at the Grouard school was taken by pneumonia.

> An Indian boy from Whitefish—he was in the next bed to me. He was coughing a
> lot—that was in February, about 1936. He got wet because he had a bad cold but
> we all had to play outside. He played in the snow and he got wet. At the time to
> go to bed—now we are in a dorm like in a hall—he was coughing and wheezing.
> I talked to the Sister—after I can talk a little bit of English, I always tried to help
> out—I said, "George is really sick Sister, what's wrong with him?" She comes
> there and I can see her make a ginger in a cup. She gave it to him and sent him to
> bed. That boy died that night about 3 o'clock in the morning.[19]

Mike Durocher, a student at Île-à-la-Crosse for nine years, said life was governed by "a regimental time clock dictated by Church functions."[20] Of the regimentation, a student from a different school said, "We were trained like dogs—clap you get up—two claps you go eat—three claps maybe you go outside."[21]

George Amato recalled that his sister once stole away from the Grouard school to attend a dance in the local town. "The priest went and caught her and brought her back and they tied her to a chair and they shaved her hair off. She hit the nun, or the Sister, and she ended up in Edmonton in a reform school for girls."[22]

One Métis student who attended the Fort Chipewyan school recalled that students who wet their beds were placed in tubs in the centre of the washroom floor and had iced water poured over their head. "That was every morning that happened and we all had to stand there and watch that. Oh my God, it was just terrible."[23] According to Robert Derocher, at Île-à-la-Crosse, bedwetters were required to "wear a diaper in front of everyone all day long."[24]

Magee Shaw recalled being physically punished "if I ever spoke or said something in my language."[25] Yvonne Lariviere, an Île-à-la-Crosse student from 1947 to 1955, recalled, "I didn't know why I was being hit because I didn't speak English. I was seven years old and I had never been hit before in my life."[26] For lapsing into the wrong language, Alphonse Janvier was made to stand holding books above his head, to stand in a corner, or to stand at the blackboard, pressing his nose within a chalk circle. He felt that he was also taught to be ashamed of his heritage: "we were taught that all Indians did was raid farmhouses, kidnap women, and burn houses."[27]

Allen Morin said that Île-à-la-Crosse was a world run by non-Aboriginal people.

> I remember the teachers used to come there from September to June, and then they'd leave, and then a new pack of teachers would come in, and they were all non-Native, and to me, I was thinking how come, how come they're coming in and leaving? And I thought, well, I guess that's because we're Indians and they're, and they're non-Native, and then only non-Natives can be teachers, or professionals, or priests, or stuff like that. And they were kind of, I think they were kind of, they separated themselves from the community, we, we didn't mingle with them.[28]

The harsh, and at times abusive, discipline was coupled with physical and sexual abuse. According to one former Île-à-la-Crosse student, "Older boys molested younger boys at night in the dormitory and priests and supervisors molested their 'favorite boys.'"[29] Clement Chartier, a student for ten years at Île-à-la-Crosse, said that "many, many of us suffered physical and sexual abuse."[30] Mike Durocher, who had been abused, said he was expelled at age fifteen for putting up posters that identified abusers. The principal called him a liar, and his parents and grandparents refused to believe his story.[31] Robert Derocher said that some staff preyed on the students' loneliness: "It seemed that he knew how to pick the, the children that were hurting and to give them any kind of attention that we were all looking for; even if it was not good."[32]

One day, Grouard school student George Amato was told that "you have to go help the Brother downstairs." According to Amato, the priest took him down "into the boiler rooms where he sat down in a chair and undid his bib overalls, pulled them down and he exposed himself, and forced me to fondle him."[33]

In the face of the hunger, discipline, and abuse, many students ran away. One student recalled, "To me that was a rough life so I proceeded to run away. I did it a few times. They took me back and I ran away again. Finally, my parents took notice that I couldn't handle it there no more. Same with my sisters there were two girls involved. So we all decided that we were not going back."[34] Colin Courtoreille was shocked by the discipline at the school in Grouard, but he could not convince his father that he was being mistreated.

My dad never saw that. He got mad at us, he said don't blame the mission because you guys gonna learn something. You're learning something, respect the Catholic way of living, like the Sisters and Fathers. Now, you're in the middle. You get a licking here and you're not gonna tell your parents because they're not going to believe you, because you're learning something.[35]

Donna Roberts, who attended the Fort Vermilion, Alberta, school for ten years, never forgot the discipline at the school.

Those that didn't follow the rules rebelled, and a few did, they got a spanking, as did the ones that ran away from the mission. I witnessed one run-away. Two boys ran away in January—dead winter, cold—they ran across the river and the priest chased them. They got as far as the middle of the river and got turned around and came back.

We witnessed it, everybody sat around the hall, and there were two of them standing up there. They were told to stand up because they were going to get a spanking right in front of all of us as an example not to run away. They got the spanking. After that, people didn't run away because they knew what they were going to get. At least a couple more times people ran away, but were always brought back.[36]

One young girl ran away from the Fort Chipewyan school when she was thirteen. Having already run away and been returned by her father, she quickly ran away again. "Dad brought me back, so I ran away again. I ran all the way from that old mission to my dad's house. I ran all the way over there with just a sweater on and this was in November." Her father took her back, asking her to stay for the year, but she ran away again before Easter.[37]

Rather than run away, some students, as they got older, fought back. Elmer Cardinal claimed that he once beat up a priest. "I beat him up pretty good; he didn't die. I kicked him in the head, I smashed his glasses and the boys gathered all around me and nobody did anything."[38]

There were also positive recollections. One former Métis student said, "I was treated well, I remember it fondly, some of those memories are the happiest of my life.... I was asked to teach some of the classes when I was older, and the teachers were sick or something. Those were happy times for me."[39] Hank Pennier, who went to the Mission, British Columbia, school in the early years of the twentieth century, spoke of how glad he was that he had been admitted to school. "As we were halfbreeds and we could not live on the reservation, we were supposed to be white and we came under the white man's status. But the priests were very kind and they made an exception in our case. They went out of their way." In fact, he regretted leaving school. One summer, he was three weeks late returning to school, in large measure because he and his brother had been waiting in their home community to be paid for work they had done for a local mill. By the time he arrived at Mission, the school was full and he could not be admitted. He was thirteen. "Things were never quite so nice again."[40] Archie Larocque, who attended the Fort Resolution school for one year, said, "The nuns were real good, they were real good, done their best." Larocque was also positive about the education he received. "They were good school teachers. They knew I was only going to be there for that one term because I was over the age limit. So they drove all they could into me. I learned quite a bit in that six or seven months."[41]

In speaking about the life at Île-à-la-Crosse, one former student, Mary Jacobson, said that although she thought the nuns treated the students well, the students were disciplined for poor performance in the classroom. Jacobson said that "we didn't learn, that is our fault if we get a licking. Because we got to try to learn and they want us to learn something."[42]

Theresa Meltenberger was proud of the fact that children at Lac La Biche took responsibility for their own entertainment.

> In the winter we built a snow fort, we had snowball fights and we played in the snow always. We had a nice yard—it would put a lot of igloos to shame. Then we had made a whole bunch of snowballs hoping that we could somehow miss somebody and hit one of the ladies there, but it never happened. Then in the summertime, we were by a lake, one of the nicest lakes, you know, before they polluted that nice beach. We'd build a raft, and in retrospect, I wonder how they got away with the lack of safety and that. You know we'd take off on the raft and the raft was a way of getting even with the one Sister we didn't like that well. It was driftwood, one side we'd had a big log and on the other, the logs got smaller. We built a seat on there for the Sister and we'd pole. Because of that large log on one side, we just moved and it upended our raft and I can still see the Sisters, they had this big starched thing around their glasses hanging on. "Oh, we're so sorry Sister," and you know, we weren't, which taught us not to be truthful all the time, I guess, but we enjoyed it.[43]

Meltenberger could recall hard work, but she also felt that she learned important skills. Although she did not like the discipline, she said, "I don't want to judge this by today's standards because the nuns most likely figured they were doing God's work you know. So who am I to assess blame to them, you know, but it took me a long time to come to terms with it."[44]

One Alberta student recalled the first-grade teacher as being "the kindest little nun that they ever had. Her name was Sister Alicia and she was really kind. She was a little old lady, I bet you she was about 70 years old and she wasn't a very tall person. I think the biggest person in our grade one class was taller than her but she was very kind." Another teacher was much tougher. "I was day dreaming, looking out the window and all of a sudden I was brought to my senses with a yardstick smashed across my back, just about where my shoulders are."[45]

Like many students, Donna Roberts developed a close and protective friendship at the St. Bruno mission in Joussard, Alberta. "We just bonded. If somebody was mean to either one of us we were sure that the other one was going to stick up for the other one. It was the mutual understanding that that was going to happen. We survived that way."[46] Angie Crerar said the only good memories she had of the years she spent at the school were the protective bonds she established with her friends. They told each other, "'You are my strength, you are my friend, you are my trust.' We tried to look after the little ones and tried to avoid some of the beatings that were not necessary. There was no such thing as respect but we taught ourselves to have respect."[47]

In other cases, students turned their anger against one another. One student said,

> You were always caged around by a big 10-foot-high fence. You're sort of caged animals, I guess. We were always fighting each other and we never got along that good. I remember three big boys, they were from up north. We had guys come all the way to our mission, it's funny, they had a residential school over there and they came to Grouard. They were all bigger boys. There was three of us would gang up on one guy. But you sure got it when they got you alone.[48]

One student who attended Saint Martin's school at Wabasca, Alberta, for eight years recalled how the bigger boys used to make the smaller boys fight. "I know I used to cry when I was fighting one guy, we didn't get along."[49]

Métis children also felt discriminated against by First Nations children. One mother said, "My kids, they didn't like school because they were mistreated. Probably could be because they were halfbreeds. They would laugh at them and things like that."[50] One student felt the same hostility from Inuit students. "One was made certain to know how you were not really, truly, an Inuk. In addition to the petty cruelties inflicted upon half-breeds for being born as such, there was the obviousness of illegitimacy."[51]

When attending the Pine Creek residential school in Manitoba, Raphael Ironstand, a boy of mixed descent who had been raised in a First Nations community, was bullied by Cree students.

> The Crees surrounded me, staring at me with hatred in their eyes, as again they called me 'Monias,' while telling me the school was for Indians only. I tried to tell them I was not a Monias, which I now knew meant white man, but a real Indian. That triggered their attack, in unison. I was kicked, punched, bitten, and my hair was pulled out by the roots. My clothes were also shredded, but the Crees suddenly disappeared, leaving me lying on the ground, bleeding and bruised.[52]

Although the sisters had showed little sympathy at the time, Ironstand had a very specific memory of a nun who showed him kindness.

> I poured out my story to this understanding nun about my confused feelings, being a non-person with white skin, even though I was an Indian. At that she put her arm around me and assured me that I was a very important person to her,

which immediately raised my self-esteem. It was the first time since I came to the school that anyone had touched me without punishing or beating me. As she ushered me out of the door, she stopped and gave me a hug, which made me feel warm all over.[53]

Such shows of affection were rare. Even if they developed close friendships, most students felt unloved. Alphonse Janvier had grown up in a household where love was present and demonstrated. "My mom hugged us a lot and my dad hugged us a lot, they spent all their time with us. After I left home, I don't ever, ever recalled [sic] ever being hugged or ever being told that I was loved. I was told that God loved me."[54] Another former Métis student from the Alberta schools spoke of how the residential schools had not taught her parents how to love, and how she had received the same joyless upbringing during the years she attended school. "There was no loving at home, no hugging, no words like 'I love you' because they were dirty words. They were taught not to show affection. The priest and nuns took that out of you. I know I was in the mission, I couldn't even talk to my brother."[55]

Because boys and girls were kept separate, families were broken up. This was a practice that continued into the 1950s. Alphonse Janvier recalled that at Île-à-la-Crosse, "you were not allowed to talk to them because this playground had an imaginary boundary that we could not cross. We talk about it now and we wonder why we had to put up with that. We used to eat in the same dormitory with a wall dividing us and two doors and we used to wave at each other and that was the only way of communication with my nieces."[56]

Children were given little preparation for the changes that their bodies would be undergoing while they were at school. One young woman, shocked when she began menstruating, went to a staff person, saying that she was bleeding to death. "She hit me so hard, she knocked me out. When I came to, she threw a rag at me and she explained what was wrong with me."[57] Magee Shaw, who attended the Grouard, Alberta, school, recalled being accused of "'fooling around with the Brothers'" when she began menstruating. She did not understand the allegation and burst into tears. Then one of the sisters "got the scissors and just chopped all one side of my hair off in front of all the kids."[58]

The government and churches sought to control the lives of former students in a variety of ways. In some cases, the schools kept female students on as paid or unpaid help after they finished their schooling. That way, they could prevent them from returning to what were perceived to be the 'corrupting' influences of their home communities, and could also arrange marriages for them. George Amato, who attended the Grouard school for nine years, said that his mother was one of the young girls who had been kept in the school. One day, the sister told her and several other girls to make themselves presentable. His mother thought that this might be because her father was coming to take her home. Instead, the girls were told to line up against a wall. "The door opened and the priest and a short white guy walked in." The man inspected the girls. "He stopped in front of my mother and put his hand on her shoulder and said, 'I'll take this one.'"[59] Similarly, the priests and nuns at Fort Chipewyan arranged a marriage for the orphan girl Martha Mercredi. Being forced into this marriage constituted her principal criticism of the school, although, in the end, she said, she was not unhappy with her marriage.[60]

Over time, there was an increase in the number of Métis people who worked at the schools. Thérèse Arcand, who became the first Métis graduate from Île-à-la-Crosse to enter the order of the Sisters of Charity, returned as the result of a bittersweet inspiration. As she prepared to leave the school in March 1929, she came across a girl who had just arrived. "She was crying. I then said to myself. 'I will go in training and come back to help my people.' That was my last thought while in Ile-à-la-Crosse."[61]

Conclusion and Calls to Action

The Métis experience of residential schooling has been overlooked for too long. It is important to recognize that Métis children attended residential schools both in southern and northern Canada. Federal government policy on Métis attendance was never consistent or consistently applied. Even during those periods in which the federal government sought to ban Métis children from the schools, church leaders continued to recruit Métis students. Because provincial governments and school boards were often unwilling to build schools in Métis communities or to allow Métis students to attend public schools, Métis parents who wished to have their children educated often had no choice but to send them to residential school. In northern Canada, the hostel system that was established in the mid-1950s placed no restrictions on the admittance of Métis children. From the 1950s onwards, many Métis children attended residential schools that were operated by provincial governments in northern and remote areas. The student experience would have varied according to time and place, as it did for all students who attended the schools. There is no denying that the harm done to the children, their parents, and the Métis community was substantial. It is an ongoing shame that this damage has not been addressed and rectified. To address these issues, the Commission has issued the following two Calls to Action in its Summary Report.

29) We call upon the parties and, in particular, the federal government, to work collaboratively with plaintiffs not included in the Indian Residential Schools Settlement Agreement to have disputed legal issues determined expeditiously on an agreed upon set of facts.

46) We call upon the parties to the Indian Residential Schools Settlement Agreement to develop and sign a Covenant of Reconciliation that would identify principles for working collaboratively to advance reconciliation in Canadian society, and that would include, but not be limited to:

   i. Reaffirmation of the parties' commitment to reconciliation.

ii. Repudiation of concepts used to justify European sovereignty over Indigenous lands and peoples, such as the Doctrine of Discovery and *terra nullius,* and the reformation of laws, governance structures, and policies within their respective institutions that continue to rely on such concepts.

iii. Full adoption and implementation of the *United Nations Declaration on the Rights of Indigenous Peoples* as the framework for reconciliation.

iv. Support for the renewal or establishment of Treaty relationships based on principles of mutual recognition, mutual respect, and shared responsibility for maintaining those relationships into the future.

v. Enabling those excluded from the Settlement Agreement to sign onto the Covenant of Reconciliation.

vi. Enabling additional parties to sign onto the Covenant of Reconciliation.

Notes

Introduction

1. McCarthy, *From the Great River*, 159–160.
2. Erickson, "Repositioning the Missionary," 132.
3. The Yukon and Alberta cases are discussed later in this chapter. For Morice, see: Gresko, "Gender and Mission," 198.
4. For an early example of this view, see: Canada, Sessional Papers 1885, number 116, volume 13, third session of the fifth Parliament, 81, Memo: Hugh Richardson, 1 December 1879.
5. For detailed treatment of the issue, see: Chartrand, Logan, and Daniels, *Métis History*.
6. Levin, "Angélique Nolin and Marguerite Nolin," 2–3; Graham, "Memorable Manitobans: Angelique Nolin (?–1869)," http://www.mhs.mb.ca/docs/people/nolin_a.shtml (accessed 14 January 2012). See also: Chaput, "Nolin, Jean-Baptiste," http://www.biographi.ca/en/bio/nolin_jean_baptiste_1826_6E.html (accessed 14 January 2012); Chartrand, "Métis Residential School Participation," 32; Daniels,"Ancestral Pain," 114; Reardon, "George Anthony Belcourt," 75–89; Lemieux, "Provencher, Joseph-Norbert," http://www.biographi.ca/en/bio/provencher_joseph_norbert_8E.html (accessed 14 January 2012).
7. Beaumont, "Origins and Influences," 167–168, 169, 183–184, 189; Library and Archives Canada, RG15-D-II-8-a, volume 1319, FIND015/31496, MIKAN no. 1499849, "Scrip affidavit for Budd, Alice, H.M., born: 19 September, 1862; father: Henry Budd; mother: Elizabeth Budd = Demande de certificat pour Budd, Alice, H.M.; né(e): le 19 septembre, 1862; père: Henry Budd; mère: Elizabeth Budd," a scrip for Henry Budd's daughter. See also: Boon, "Budd, Henry," http://www.biographi.ca/en/bio/budd_henry_10E.html (accessed 5 December 2011); Thomas, "Settee, James," http://www.biographi.ca/en/bio/settee_james_13E.html (accessed 9 December 2011); West, *Substance of a journal*, 96; Hudson's Bay Company Archives Biographical Sheets, "Hope, James," http://www.gov.mb.ca/chc/archives/hbca/biographical/h/hope_james.pdf (accessed 19 January 2012); Stevenson, "The Red River Indian Mission School," 129–165; Stevenson, "Journals and Voices," 41.
8. Prud'homme, "The Life and Times of Archbishop Taché," http://www.mhs.mb.ca/docs/transactions/3/tache.shtml (accessed 28 January 2012); Erickson, "Repositioning the Missionary," 120.
9. Van West, "Acculturation by Design," 93.
10. Erickson, "Repositioning the Missionary," 115–116.

Student lives

1. Bird, *Living Kindness,* 5.
2. Bird, *Living Kindness,* 10.
3. Bird, *Living Kindness,* 7–8.
4. Bird, *Living Kindness,* 11.
5. Bird, *Living Kindness,* 11.
6. Bird, *Living Kindness,* 13.
7. Bird, *Living Kindness,* 13.
8. Bird, *Living Kindness,* 19.
9. Bird, *Living Kindness,* 21.
10. Bird, *Living Kindness,* 20.
11. Bird, *Living Kindness,* 24.
12. Bird, *Living Kindness,* 34.
13. Bird, *Living Kindness,* 85.
14. Bird, *Living Kindness,* 87.
15. Bird, *Living Kindness,* 79.
16. Bird, *Living Kindness,* 81.
17. Campbell, *Halfbreed,* 12–13; *Encyclopedia of Immigration, Dominion Lands Act (Canada) (1872),* http://immigration-online.org/88-dominion-lands-act-canada-1872.html (accessed 12 July 2013).
18. Campbell, *Halfbreed,* 17.
19. Campbell, *Halfbreed,* 14–15, 18.
20. Campbell, *Halfbreed,* 31.
21. Campbell, *Halfbreed,* 44.
22. Campbell, *Halfbreed,* 44.
23. Campbell, *Halfbreed,* 46.
24. Campbell, *Halfbreed,* 46.
25. Campbell, *Halfbreed,* 77.
26. Campbell, *Halfbreed,* 47.
27. Dempsey, *Gentle Persuader,* 1–10, 21.
28. Dempsey, *Gentle Persuader,* 12.
29. Dempsey, *Gentle Persuader,* 14.
30. Gladstone, "Indian School Days," 19.
31. Dempsey, *Gentle Persuader,* 16–17.
32. Dempsey, *Gentle Persuader,* 19.
33. Gladstone, "Indian School Days," 21–22.
34. Gladstone, "Indian School Days," 22.
35. Gladstone, "Indian School Days," 22–23.
36. Dempsey, *Gentle Persuader,* 37, 53–60.

The Métis and the early residential school system: 1883–1910

1. Davin, *Report on Industrial Schools*, 9.
2. Flanagan, "Hugh Richardson," http://www.biographi.ca/en/bio/richardson_hugh_1826_1913_14E.html (accessed 1 August 2012).
3. Canada, Sessional Papers 1885, number 116, volume 13, third session of the fifth Parliament, 81, Memo: Hugh Richardson, 1 December 1879.
4. Library and Archives Canada, RG10, volume 3674, file 11422-1, E. Dewdney to the Superintendent General Indian Affairs, 10 November 1884.
5. Huel, *Proclaiming the Gospel,* 130.
6. TRC, NRA, Library and Archives Canada, RG10, volume 3675, file 11422-4, E. Dewdney to Superintendent General of Indian Affairs, 27 February 1886. [PLD-009190]
7. Canada, *Annual Report of the Department of Indian Affairs, 1893*, 114.
8. Canada, *Annual Report of the Department of Indian Affairs, 1889*, 120.
9. Marceau-Kozicki, "Onion Lake Residential Schools," 60.
10. TRC, NRA, Library and Archives Canada, RG10, volume 6320, file 658-1, part 1, J. R. Matheson to Hayter Reed, 18 February 1895. [PAR-003580-0001]
11. Marceau-Kozicki, "Onion Lake Residential Schools," 60–61.
12. Marceau-Kozicki, "Onion Lake Residential Schools," 63.
13. Redford, "Attendance at Indian Residential Schools," 38.
14. Canada, *Annual Report of the Department of Indian Affairs, 1893*, 247.
15. TRC, NRA, Library and Archives Canada, RG10, volume 6255, file 576-1, part 1, John Semmens to E. McColl, 4 April 1895. [BRS-000177]
16. Canada, *Annual Report of the Department of Indian Affairs, 1898*, 332.
17. Library and Archives Canada, RG10, volume 6031, "Headquarters – Admission of Half-breeds to Residential Schools," Saskatchewan and Calgary School Division, letter, to the Department of Indian Affairs (21 July 1896), quoted in Logan, "Lost Generations," 71.
18. Canada, *Annual Report of the Department of Indian Affairs, 1899,* 356.
19. Library and Archives Canada, RG10, volume 6031, "Extract from a letter dated the 19th July, 1899, from the Re. Father Hugonard."
20. Carney, "Relations in Education," 32; McCarthy, *From the Great River*, 174–175.
21. TRC, NRA, Library and Archives Canada, RG10, volume 3952, file 134858, E. Grouard to Prime Minister, 1 October 1900. [FPU-001900]
22. TRC, NRA, Library and Archives Canada, R776-0-5 (RG55), volume 562, T.B. #252440, Clifford Sifton to Mr. Smart, 18 October 1899. [NPC-523981c]
23. Drouin, *Joyau dans la plaine*, 4–7; Devine, *People Who Own Themselves*, 184. See also: Pocklington, *Government and Politics*, 8.
24. Library and Archives Canada, RG15, D-II-1, volume 708, file 366530, part 1, Albert Lacombe, "A Philanthropic Plan to Redeem the Half-Breeds of Manitoba and the Northwest Territories."
25. Library and Archives Canada, RG15, D-II-1, volume 708, file 360530, PC Number 3723, "Extract from a Report of the Committee of the Honourable the Privy Council, approved by His Excellency on the 28th December, 1895; Annex "A" to P.C. Number 3723, 12 December 1895.
26. Stanley, "Alberta's Half-Breed Reserve," 82.
27. Stanley, "Alberta's Half-Breed Reserve," 83.
28. Library and Archives Canada, RG15, volume 708, file 360-530, "To My Dear Children and Friends Half-Breeds of Manitoba and the North-West," A. Lacombe.

29. Stanley, "Alberta's Half-Breed Reserve," 84–87, 88n45; Metis Association of Alberta, et al., *Metis Land Rights*, 168, 170.

30. Library and Archives Canada, RG10, volume 3984, file 167719-1, FIND010/25053, MIKAN no. 2058744, J. A. Thérien to Smart, 17 February 1898.

31. Library and Archives Canada, RG10, volume 3984, file 167719-1, FIND010/25053, MIKAN no. 2058744, J. A. Thérien to Smart, 17 February 1898.

32. Library and Archives Canada, LG15, volume 708, D-II-1, file 360530, J. E. Thérien to C. Sifton, 1 February 1901.

33. Library and Archives Canada, RG10, volume 3984, file 167719-1, FIND010/25053, MIKAN no. 2058744, H. C. Ross to the Secretary, 9 March 1898.

34. Library and Archives Canada, RG15, D-II-1, volume 708, file 360530, J. Smart to F. Pedley, 13 October 1898; A. A. Ruttan to The Secretary, Department of Interior, January 1899.

35. Library and Archives Canada, RG15, D-II-1, volume 708, file 360530, J. E. Thérien to C. Sifton, 1 February 1901.

36. Stanley, "Alberta's Half-Breed Reserve," 86–87.

37. Stanley, "Alberta's Half-Breed Reserve," 93.

38. Oblates of Mary Immaculate Lacombe Canada, Grandin Province Archives, Acc. 71.200, box 132, file 5737, Louis Guillaume to Father Provincial, 12 April 1942.

39. Stanley, "Alberta's Half-Breed Reserve," 98.

40. Oblates of Mary Immaculate Lacombe Canada, Grandin Province Archives, Acc. 71.200, box 132, file 5737, Louis Guillaume to Father Provincial, 12 April 1942.

41. Stanley, "Alberta's Half-Breed Reserve," 100–104.

Forty years of haphazard policy: 1899–1937

1. Library and Archives Canada, RG10, volume 3931, file 117377-1C, D. Laird to Secretary, Indian Affairs, 15 August 1900.

2. TRC, NRA, Library and Archives Canada, RG10, volume 6197, file 465-1, part 1, Martin Benson to Deputy Superintendent General, Indian Affairs, 30 November 1906. [KNR-000624]

3. TRC, NRA, Library and Archives Canada, RG10, volume 6197, file 465-1, part 1, J. D. McLean to the Principal of the Kenora Boarding School, 7 January 1907. [KNR-000628]

4. Library and Archives Canada, RG10, volume 6031, file 150-9, part 1, Extract from memorandum of D. C. Scott, Accountant Dated December 11, 1906, to Deputy Superintendent General, Relative to the Admission of Half-Breeds to Indian Schools.

5. Library and Archives Canada, RG10, volume 6320, file 658-1, part 1, Microfilm reel C-9802, M. Benson to Deputy Superintendent General, Indian Affairs, 6 May 1906. [120.00280]

6. Titley, "Dunbow Indian Industrial School," 104.

7. Titley, "Dunbow Indian Industrial School," 107–108.

8. United Church Archives, A. Sutherland Papers, Prairie provinces Indian missions, Red Deer Industrial School, January–March 1909, A. Barner, Principal, box 134, A. Barner to A. Sutherland, 24 March 1909, quoted in Fox, "Failure of Red Deer Industrial School," 92.

9. United Church Archives, A. Sutherland Papers, Prairie provinces, Indian missions, Red Deer Industrial School, April 1909–1910, A. Barner, Principal, box 135, D. C. Scott to A. Sutherland, 10 May 1909, quoted in Fox, "Failure of Red Deer Industrial School," 92.

10. Canada, *Annual Report of the Department of Indian Affairs, 1910,* 273–274.

11. TRC, NRA, Library and Archives Canada, RG10, volume 6039, file 160-1, part 1, "Agreement in Regard to the Management of Indian Boarding Schools and Correspondence Relating Thereto, 1911," 7. [UCA-080784]

12. TRC, NRA, Library and Archives Canada, RG10, volume 6327, file 660-1, part 1, J. D. McLean to J. A. Calder, 18 January 1911. [PLD-007440]

13. Library and Archives Canada, RG10, volume 7184, file 1/25-1-5-7, part 1, Assistant Deputy and Secretary to Indian Agents, 20 March 1911.

14. Library and Archives Canada, RG10, volume 7184, file 1/25-1-5-7, part 1, J. P. G. Day, to D. McLean, 31 March 1911.

15. Library and Archives Canada, RG10, volume 6031, file 150-9, part 1, J. A. J. McKenna, 9 November 1911.

16. Canada, *Annual Report of the Department of Indian Affairs, 1912*, 539.

17. Library and Archives Canada, RG10, volume 6031, file 150-9, part 1, Frank Pedley to Mr. Rogers, 2 May 1912.

18. Huel, *Proclaiming the Gospel,* 161.

19. Moine, *My Life in a Residential School*, n.p.

20. Moine, *My Life in a Residential School*, n.p.

21. TRC, NRA, Library and Archives Canada, RG10, volume 6327, file 660-1, part 1, J. Hugonnard to The Secretary, Indian Affairs, 18 January 1913. [PLD-007446]

22. TRC, NRA, Headquarters 777/25-1-007, 02/13–03/65, volume 1, HQ, E. Grouard to Superintendent General, Indian Affairs, 18 January 1913. [JRD-000206]

23. Library and Archives Canada, RG10, volume 6031, file 150-9, part 1, Duncan Campbell Scott, memorandum, 16 October 1913.

24. Devine, *People Who Own Themselves*, 172–174.

25. Marceau-Kozicki, "Onion Lake Residential Schools," 137–138.

26. TRC, NRA, Library and Archives Canada, RG10, volume 6300, file 650-1, part 1, Augustus Ball to Indian Affairs, 1 June 1908. [BVL-000794]

27. TRC, NRA, Library and Archives Canada, RG10, volume 6300, file 650-1, part 1, Assistant Deputy and Secretary to Augustus Ball, 14 June 1918. [BVL-000795]

28. Library and Archives Canada, RG10, volume 6031, file 150-9, part 1, W. M. Graham, to Duncan Scott, 29 October 1921.

29. Canada, *Annual Report of the Department of Indian Affairs, 1921*, 27.

30. See: Obituary, "St. Pierre–Mrs. Mary," http://baileysfuneralhome.com/book-of-memories/1488588/Pierre-Mary/obituary.php?Printable=true.

31. Mary St. Pierre, quoted in interview, "Norm Fleury (NF) Interview – Mary St. Pierre," http://www.metismuseum.ca/resource.php/01194, 2.

32. Mary St. Pierre, quoted in interview, "Norm Fleury (NF) Interview – Mary St. Pierre," http://www.metismuseum.ca/resource.php/01194, 2–3.

33. TRC, NRA, Library and Archives Canada, RG10, volume 6300, file 650-1, part 1, A. F. MacKenzie to Reverend M. Lajeunesse, 17 September 1925. [200.4.00023]

34. TRC, NRA, Library and Archives Canada, RG10, volume 6300, file 650-1, part 1, Martin Lajeunesse to A. F. MacKenzie, 17 October 1925. [BVL-000867]

35. TRC, NRA, Library and Archives Canada, RG10, volume 6300, file 650-1, part 1, J. D. McLean to Reverend M. Lajeunesse, 17 September 1925. [BVL-000869-0001]

36. TRC, NRA, Library and Archives Canada, RG10, volume 6300, file 650-1, part 1, J. D. McLean to Reverend M. Adam, 17 December 1928. [BVL-000894]

37. TRC, NRA, Library and Archives Canada, RG10, volume 6300, file 650-1, part 1, Martin Lajeunesse, Memorandum, Re: Admission of Half-breed children into the school, 21 January 1929. [BVL-000896]

38. Provincial Archives of Alberta, Oblates of Mary Immaculate, Pariosses noninventoriées: Brocket Correspondence 1922–29, Christianson to Le Vern (28 August 1934), quoted in Huel, *Proclaiming the Gospel*, 162.

39. TRC, NRA, Library and Archives Canada, RG10, volume 6323, file 658-10, part 3, W. M. Graham to Secretary Indian Affairs, 16 December 1929. [PAR-020862]

40. Library and Archives Canada, RG10, volume 6323, file 658-10, part 3, W. M. Graham to the Secretary of the Department of Indian Affairs, 5 December 1929.

41. Marceau-Kozicki, "Onion Lake Residential Schools," 174.

42. Library and Archives Canada, RG10, volume 6031, file 159-9, part 1, Duncan C. Scott to Father Rieu, 31 May 1930.

43. TRC, NRA, No document location, no document file source, Bishop of Grouard to J. J. McLellan, 3 March 1935. [GMA-005047]

44. TRC, NRA, Library and Archives Canada, RG10, volume 6258, file 576-10, part 9, D. Robinson to T. A. Crerar, 20 February 1936. [NCA-011510-0001]

45. TRC, NRA, Library and Archives Canada, RG10, volume 6258, file 576-10, part 9, A. F. MacKenzie to D. Robinson, 10 March 1936. [AEMR-010749]

46. Provincial Archives of Alberta, AN 75.75, box 2, file 8:23, Malcolm Norris, quoted in Daniels, "Ancestral Pain," 141.

47. Wall, "Joseph Francis Dion," http://www.ualberta.ca/~walld/dion.html (accessed 23 March 2012).

48. "Alberta Métis Settlements," http://www.ualberta.ca/~walld/ab2introsketch.html (accessed 23 March 2012).

49. Dobbin, *One and a Half Men*, 91–100.

50. "Reports, Evidence, etc., re: the Report of the Royal Commission to Investigate the Conditions of the Half-Breed Population of Alberta, Edmonton, Department of Lands and Forest, 1935, 543," quoted in Dobbin, *One and a Half Men*, 100.

51. Alberta and Ewing, *Report of the Royal Commission*, 6–7.

52. *Report of the Royal Commission Appointed to Investigate the Conditions of the Half-Breed Population of Alberta*, 1936, 6–7, as quoted in Chartrand, "Métis Residential School Participation," 41.

53. Alberta and Ewing, *Report of the Royal Commission*, 11–14.

54. Martin, "Alberta Métis Settlements," 360–361.

55. Pocklington, *Government and Politics*, 73.

56. Pocklington, *Government and Politics*, 25–26.

57. TRC, NRA, Library and Archives Canada, RG85, volume 938, file 12497, St. Paul's Hostel – Dawson Yukon Territory, 1941–1943, T. R. L. MacInnes to Inspectors, Indian Agents, and Principals of Residential Schools, 10 December 1937. [DAW-000024]

58. Library and Archives Canada, RG85, volume 938, file 12497, St. Paul's Hostel – Dawson Yukon Territory, 1941–1943, T. R. L. MacInnes to Inspectors, Indian Agents, and Principals of Residential Schools, 10 December 1937. [DAW-000024]

Île-à-la-Crosse

1. Armour, "Henry, Alexander," http://www.biographi.ca/en/bio/henry_alexander_1739_1824_6E.html (accessed 30 December 2011); McLennan, "Ile-a-la-Crosse," http://esask.uregina.ca/entry/ile-a-la-crosse.html (accessed 4 November 2014).

2. Foster, "Auld, William," http://www.biographi.ca/en/bio/auld_william_6E.html (accessed 24 December 2011).

3. Champagne, *Les missions catholiques,* 78n28; Foran, "Les Gens de Cette Place," 36–37.

4. Foran, "Les Gens de Cette Place," 105–106, 203.

5. McLennan, "Ile-a-la-Crosse," http://esask.uregina.ca/entry/ile-a-la-crosse.html (accessed 22 December 2011); Foran, "Les Gens de Cette Place," 41; "Chateau Saint-Jean ... Black Robes and Grey Dresses," [part 1], Memories of Deep River website, http://www.jkcc.com/robes.html (accessed 1 January 2012).

6. "Arrival of the Grey Nuns," Memories of Deep River website, http://www.jkcc.com/rcnuns.html (accessed 23 December 2011).

7. Library and Archives Canada, RG10, volume 3666, file 10125, "Ile-a-la-Crosse Agency – Reverend Mr. Legard's [sic: Legeard's] Report on the School at Ile-a-la Crosse," (1878), items 2, 8, copy of a letter from Prosper Legeard, Ile a la Crosse, 25 March 1878, to David Laird, Lieutenant Governor NWT, at Battleford.

8. Foran, "Les Gens de Cette Place," 57, 58. See also: "Arrival of the Grey Nuns," http://www.jkcc.com/rcnuns.html (accessed 23 December 2011).

9. Foran, "Les Gens de Cette Place," 185–187.

10. Foran, "Les Gens de Cette Place," 60.

11. Foran, "Les Gens de Cette Place," 151–152.

12. Canada, *Annual Report of the Department of Indian Affairs, 1882,* 213; LAC, RG10, volume 3666, "Ile-a-la-Crosse Agency – Reverend Mr. Legard's Report," item 3. The first supervisor of the resident boys was Oblate lay brother Louis Dubé.

13. Foran, "Les Gens de Cette Place," 154.

14. Foran, "Les Gens de Cette Place," 156.

15. Foran, "Les Gens de Cette Place," 157.

16. Foran, "Les Gens de Cette Place," 74, 118, 124, 125, 127, 157–158, 161.

17. Foran, "Les Gens de Cette Place," 158.

18. Library and Archives Canada, RG10, volume 3666, "Ile-a-la-Crosse Agency – Reverend Mr. Legard's Report," item 3, 4; "Arrival of the Grey Nuns," http://www.jkcc.com/rcnuns.html (accessed 23 December 2011).

19. Foran, "Les Gens de Cette Place," 183.

20. Foran, "Les Gens de Cette Place," 183–184.

21. Library and Archives Canada, RG10, volume 3666, "Ile-a-la-Crosse Agency – Reverend Mr. Legard's Report," items, 10.

22. Foran, "Les Gens de Cette Place," 187–188.

23. Foran, "Les Gens de Cette Place," 161.

24. Provincial Archives of Manitoba, Riel Papers, Sara Riel to Louis Riel, 6 August 1874, quoted in Erickson, "'Bury Our Sorrows,'" 34–35.

25. Erickson, "'Bury Our Sorrows,'" 33, 38.

26. Canada, *Annual Report of the Department of Indian Affairs, 1883,* 180–181.

27. Foran, "Les Gens de Cette Place," 193.

28. Canada, *Annual Report of the Department of Indian Affairs, 1908*. Part II, page 54, in a table, identifies Lac la Plonge as "Formerly the Ile à la Crosse boarding school."

29. "Chateau Saint-Jean," part 1, http://www.jkcc.com/robes.html (accessed 1 January 2012); "Arrival of the Grey Nuns," http://www.jkcc.com/rcnuns.html (accessed 23 December 2011).

30. "Chateau Saint-Jean," part 1, http://www.jkcc.com/robes.html (accessed 1 January 2012).

31. "Chateau Saint-Jean," part 1, http://www.jkcc.com/robes.html (accessed 1 January 2012).

32. Arcand, quoted in "Les Metisse," part 2, http://www.jkcc.com/motherstwo.html (accessed 1 January 2012).

33. Lariviere and Arcand, quoted in "Les Metisse," http://www.jkcc.com/motherstwo.html (accessed 1 January 2012).

34. Arcand, quoted in "Les Metisse," part 2, http://www.jkcc.com/motherstwo.html (accessed 1 January 2012).

35. Arcand, quoted in "Les Metisse," part 2, http://www.jkcc.com/motherstwo.html (accessed 1 January 2012).

36. "Arrival of the Grey Nuns," http://www.jkcc.com/rcnuns.html (accessed 23 December 2011).

37. "Arrival of the Grey Nuns," http://www.jkcc.com/rcnuns.html (accessed 23 December 2011).

38. Quiring, *CCF Colonialism*, 242–244; Barron, *Walking in Indian Moccasins*, 159.

39. "Arrival of the Grey Nuns," http://www.jkcc.com/rcnuns.html (accessed 23 December 2011).

40. "Hospital Buildings and Health Care," http://www.jkcc.com/rchospital.html (accessed 6 January 2012); "Arrival of the Grey Nuns," http://www.jkcc.com/rcnuns.html (accessed 23 December 2011).

41. Quiring, *CCF Colonialism*, 244.

42. "Hospital Buildings and Health Care," http://www.jkcc.com/rchospital.html (accessed 6 January 2012); "Arrival of the Grey Nuns," http://www.jkcc.com/rcnuns.html (accessed 23 December 2011); "History of Language Instructions in Ile-a-la-Crosse, Saskatchewan," Sakitawak Cultural Site, http://216.174.135.221/michif/michiflanguage.html (accessed 3 January 2012).

43. Blakeney, *An Honourable Calling*, 110; "Ile-A-La-Crosse celebrates Bi-Centennial, Courtesy of 'DENOSA,'" http://www.jkcc.com/invaintwo.html (accessed 6 January 2012).

Métis residential school education in the North

1. Carney, "Relations in Education," 280–284.

2. Coates and Morrison, *Land of the Midnight Sun*, 219–220 (for examples of church provision of education, see: 213–215, 220).

3. Coates, "'Betwixt and Between,'" 151–152.

4. Peake, *Bishop Who Ate His Boots*, 106, 108.

5. TRC, NRA, Anglican Diocese of Yukon Fonds, Yukon Archives, COR 255, file 15, series 1.1, Anglican Church, W. W. Williams to Bishop, 18 July 1919. [DAW-000449]

6. Peake, *Bishop Who Ate His Boots*, 108.

7. TRC, NRA, Library and Archives Canada, RG10, volume 6481, file 941-1, part 1, Isaac Stringer to Duncan C. Scott, 31 January 1922. [DAW-000274]

8. TRC, NRA, Library and Archives Canada, RG10, volume 6481, file 941-1, part 1, General Secretary Missionary Society of the Church of England in Canada to D. C. Scott, 15 September 1922. [DAW-000288]

9. TRC, NRA, Library and Archives Canada, RG10, volume 6481, file 941-1, part 1, Clerk of the Privy Council, Report of the Committee of the Privy Council, 11 January 1923. [DAW-000300]

10. TRC, NRA, Anglican Diocese of Yukon Fonds, Yukon Archives, COR 253, file 14, series 1.1, Anglican Church, I. O. Stringer to E. J. Naftel, 7 August 1923. [DAW-000443]

11. TRC, NRA, Library and Archives Canada, RG10, volume 6481, file 941-1, part 1, John Hawksley to J. D. McLean, 4 October 1922. [DAW-000289]

12. TRC, NRA, Anglican Diocese of Yukon Fonds, Yukon Archives, COR 253, file 14, series 1.1, Anglican Church, C. F. Johnson to I. O. Stringer, 6 September 1926. [DAW-000251-0004]

13. TRC, NRA, Anglican Diocese of Yukon Fonds, Yukon Archives, COR 253, file 14, series 1.1, Anglican Church, C. F. Johnson to I. O. Stringer, 3 October 1926; [DAW-000251-0005] I. O. Stringer to C. F. Johnson, 28 December 1926. [DAW-000251-0008]

14. TRC, NRA, Anglican Diocese of Yukon Fonds, Yukon Archives, file 11, volume 3, Dawson City Hostel, 1922–1934, Anglican Church –Diocese of Yukon Records, COR 252, [box 4] series 1-1A, C. F. Johnson to I. O. Stringer, 3 October 1927. [DAW-000251-0015]

15. TRC, NRA, Anglican Diocese of Yukon Fonds, Yukon Archives, file 11, volume 3, Dawson City Hostel, 1922–1934, Anglican Church – Diocese of Yukon Records, COR 252, [box 4] series 1-1A, C. F. Johnson to I. O. Stringer, 25 November 1927. [DAW-000251-0018]

16. TRC, NRA, Library and Archives Canada – Ottawa, file 10227, Institutionalization in St. Paul's Hostel, Dawson, Yukon Territory, 1939, FA 85-44, Perm. volume 902, Royal Canadian Mounted Police Report, W. W. Sutherland, 5 June 1939. [DAW-000550-0003]

17. TRC, NRA, Library and Archives Canada, RG85, volume 938, file 12497, St. Paul's Hostel – Dawson Yukon Territory, 1941–1943, R. A. Hoey to Harold McGill, 23 January 1942. [DAW-000027-0001]

18. TRC, NRA, Library and Archives Canada, RG85, volume 938, file 12497, St. Paul's Hostel – Dawson Yukon Territory, 1941–1943, R. A. Gibson to J. A. Jackell, 19 March 1942. [DAW-000032]

19. TRC, NRA, Library and Archives Canada, RG85, volume 938, file 12497, St. Paul's Hostel – Dawson Yukon Territory, 1941–1943, J. A. Jackell to R. A. Gibson, 24 July 1942; [DAW-000037] Bureau of Northwest Territories and Yukon Affairs, Memorandum to Mr. Cumming, 5 May 1943. [DAW-000053]

20. TRC, NRA, Anglican Diocese of Yukon Fonds, Yukon Archives, COR 295, F. 2, 1944–1952, series III.3.c, Anglican Church, Diocese of the Yukon Records, Matron to Miss E. Adams, 15 March 1949. [DAW-000133]

21. TRC, NRA, Anglican Diocese of Yukon Fonds, Yukon Archives, COR 295, F. 4, 1946–1952, series III.3.c, Anglican Church, Diocese of the Yukon Records, Unsigned letter to B. Catteral, 14 January 1952. [DAW-000204]

22. TRC, NRA, St Paul's Hostel, Dawson City, Yukon TC, IAP Hostel Narrative, n.d., 9. [Nar-000077]

23. TRC, NRA, Anglican Diocese of Yukon Fonds, Yukon Archives, COR 295, F. 2, 1944–1952, series III.3.c, Anglican Church, Diocese of the Yukon Records, [illegible] to A. H. Gibson, 18 October 1950. [DAW-000172]

24. TRC, NRA, Library and Archives Canada, RG10, volume 8762, file 906/25-1-001, R. J. Meek to Indian Affairs Branch, 4 February 1954. [YKS-000750]

25. TRC, NRA, Anglican Diocese of Yukon Fonds, Yukon Archives, COR 295, F. 4, 1946–1952, series III.3.c, Anglican Church, Diocese of the Yukon Records, Unsigned letter to B. Catteral, 14 January 1952. [DAW-000204]

26. TRC, NRA, Anglican Church of Canada, General Synod Archives, Northern Lights, Anglican Church of Canada, *Northern Lights,* Number 2, New Edition, May 1953, 3–4. [DYK-201507]

27. TRC, NRA, Anglican Church of Canada, General Synod Archives, Northern Lights, Anglican Church of Canada, "Something Attempted," *Northern Lights,* Number 6, New Edition, November 1954, 3. [DYK-201511] For origins as army hut, see: "Fire Completely Destroys St. Agnes Hostel," *Northern Lights*, Number 40, Spring 1947, 20. [DYK-201546]

28. TRC, NRA, Library and Archives Canada, RG85, volume 1241, file 311/200-G, part 3, School Buildings – Whitehorse, Y.T., [Construction and Maintenance], 1954–1955, Harry Thompson, Report to W. G. Brown, Commissioner of the Yukon Territory, on Dormitory Accommodation in Whitehorse for Yukon School Children, 7 May 1955. [BAP-001338]

29. TRC, NRA, Anglican Diocese of Yukon Fonds, Yukon Archives, file 3, Indian Department, 1946–1959, Anglican Church – Diocese of Yukon Records [box 14], series I-I-1.c, folder 3 of 18, COR 262, Unsigned Anglican report, 7 April 1955. [DYK-010139]

30. TRC, NRA, Anglican Church of Canada, General Synod Archives, Northern Lights, "Clara Tizya, Life Member," *Northern Lights*, Number 38, Summer 1966, 10. [DYK-201544]

31. TRC, NRA, INAC – Resolution Sector – IRS Historical Files Collection – Ottawa, 853/1-13, 1965–1967, volume 2, E. W. Johnson to Mrs. J. Lumley, 19 July 1966. [YKS-003122]

32. TRC, NRA, Library and Archives Canada, RG85, Perm. volume 1877, file 630/101-3, part 1, R.C. School Day Resolution, 1905–1944, FA 85-8, G. Breynat to O. S. Finnie, 30 June 1921. [RCN-001564-0008]

33. TRC, NRA, Library and Archives Canada, RG85, Perm. volume 1877, file 630/101-3, part 1, R.C. School Day Resolution, 1905–1944, FA 85-8, Duncan Campbell Scott to J. P. Dunne, 30 September 1921. [RCN-001565-0000]

34. TRC, NRA, Library and Archives Canada, RG10, volume 6475, file 918-1, part 1, O. S. Finnie to N. W. Cory, 17 August 1921. [FPU-000092] For creation of the Northwest Territories Branch and Finnie's position as director, see: Dickerson, *Whose North?*, 31.

35. Carney, "Relations in Education," 223, 254.

36. Carney, "Relations in Education," 239.

37. TRC, NRA, Library and Archives Canada, RG85, Perm. volume 1879, file 630/109-2, part 2, Indian Boarding School/Hay River/St. Peter's Mission Day School, 1924–1932, FA 85-8, J. D. McLean to A. J. Vale, 17 December 1925. [HRU-000391-0001]

38. TRC, NRA, Library and Archives Canada, RG85, Perm. volume 1877, file 630/101-3, part 1, R.C. School Day Resolution, 1905–1944, FA 85-8, G. Breynat to O. S. Finnie, 22 January 1929. [RCN-001598-0004]

39. TRC, NRA, Library and Archives Canada, RG85, Perm. volume 1877, file 630/101-3, part 1, R.C. School Day Resolution, 1905–1944, FA 85-8, O. S. Finnie to D. C. Scott, 19 February 1929. [RCN-001598-0000]

40. TRC, NRA, Library and Archives Canada – Ottawa, RG85, Perm. volume 1877, file 630/101-3, part 1, R.C. School Day Resolution, 1905–1944, FA 85-8, Chairman, Dominion Lands Board, Department of the Interior, Dominion Lands Administration to H. H. Rowatt, 23 September 1933. [RCN-001623-0001]

41. TRC, NRA, Library and Archives Canada, RG85, volume 1505, file 600-1-1, part 1, N.W.T. – General Policy File – Education and Schools, 1905–1944, J. Turner to R. A. Gibson, 15 February 1935. [FRU-000540]

42. TRC, NRA, Library and Archives Canada, RG85, Perm. volume 1883, file 630/219-2, part 3, Shingle Point Anglican School 1935–1936, FA 85-8, R. A. Gibson to J. Lorne Turner, 28 February 1935. [SPU-000278]

43. TRC, NRA, Library and Archives Canada – Ottawa, RG85, Perm. volume 1877, file 630/101-3, part 1, R.C. School Day Resolution, 1905–1944, FA 85-8, Bishop G. Breynat to Roy A. Gibson, 30 June 1941. [RCN-001697-0002]

44. TRC, NRA, Library and Archives Canada – Ottawa, RG85, Perm. volume 1877, file 630/101-3, part 1, R.C. School Day Resolution, 1905–1944, FA 85-8, R. A. Gibson to G. Breynat, 4 July 1941. [RCN-001697-0001]

45. Fumoleau, *As Long as This Land Shall Last,* 368.

46. TRC, NRA, RG85, volume 225, file 630/118-1, part 1, Government School – Fort McPherson – N.W.T., 1900–1950, A. L. Fleming to R. A. Gibson, 15 May 1944. [ASU-001449]

Provincial responsibility: 1940–1960

1. Saskatchewan Archives Board Education File, Add 2 file #48; Correspondence, Re: Metis, Saskatoon, University of Saskatchewan, quoted in Logan, "We Were Outsiders," 68.

2. Saskatchewan Archives Board Education File, Add 2 file #48; Correspondence, Re: Metis, Saskatoon, University of Saskatchewan, quoted in Logan, "We Were Outsiders," 67.

3. Barron, *Walking in Indian Moccasins,* 17–19.

4. TRC, NRA, Archdiocese of Grouard-McLennan, Fort Vermilion file 0463, N. P. L'Heureux to J. Huguerre, 24 January 1940. [GMA-000463]

5. TRC, NRA, Library and Archives Canada, RG10, volume 6377, file 766-10, part 2, C. Pant Schmidt to Secretary, Indian Affairs, 31 January 1940. [FTV-005479]

6. TRC, NRA, Library and Archives Canada, RG10, volume 6377, file 766-10, part 2, Excerpt from letter of Doctor H. A. Hamman, Fort Vermilion, dated January 20, 1940. [FTV-071121-0001]

7. TRC, NRA, Library and Archives Canada, RG10, volume 6314, file 655-10, part 1, Samuel Lovell to Secretary Indian Affairs, 11 April 1940. [GUY-000105]

8. TRC, NRA, Library and Archives Canada, RG10, volume 6314, file 655-10, part 1, Philip Phelan to S. Lovell, 18 April 1940. [GUY-051716]

9. TRC, NRA, Library and Archives Canada, RG10, volume 6254, file 575-10, part 3, Philip Phelan to A. G. Smith, 19 September 1946. [BIR-006280]

10. TRC, NRA, Library and Archives Canada, RG10, volume 6279, file 584-10, part 4, R. S. Davis to Indian Affairs, 30 August 1951. [SBR-110937]

11. TRC, NRA, Library and Archives Canada, RG29, volume 2367, file 264-15-4, part 1, R. B. Curry to H. C. L. Gillman, 8 June 1955. [MER-003420]

12. TRC, NRA, Archdiocese of Grouard-McLennan, 0200B, W. E. Frame to Henri Routhier, 2 May 1946. [GMA-000200-0002]

13. TRC, NRA, No document location, no document file source, Henri Routhier to W. E. Frame, 30 April 1946. [GMA-002184-0000]

14. TRC, NRA, Library and Archives Canada, 205/25-1, volume II, 06/48–12/55 NAC, G. H. Gooderham to B. F. Neary, 28 January 1950. [RCA-001909]

15. TRC, NRA, Archdiocese of Grouard-McLennan, 5556, Henri Routhier to C. B. Hill, 11 June 1950. [GMA-005556]

16. TRC, NRA, No document location, no document file source, Waller, Regional School Inspector, Extracts from Inspection Report of Regional School Inspector Waller regarding his inspection of the Grouard Indian Residential School, on June 4 and June 5th, 1951. [GMA-000221-0001]

17. TRC, NRA, No document location, no document file source, Philip Phelan to Bishop Henri Routhier, 19 October 1951. [GMA-001509-0001]

18. TRC, NRA, No document location, no document file source, Henri Routhier to R. F. Davey, 20 February 1954. [GMA-001549]

19. TRC, NRA, Library and Archives Canada, RG10, volume 8759, file 779/25-1, volume 1, Reverend E. Filion to P. G. Conrad, 15 January 1959. [SMD-014051-0003]

20. TRC, NRA, No document location, no document file source, Mgr Routhier to Oscar Fadum, 2 March 1959. [GMA-000243-0002]

21. Chalmers, "Northland," 5.

22. Chalmers, "Northland," 7.

23. Chalmers, "Northland," 27–31.

24. Blakeney, *An Honourable Calling*, 110.

25. Frontier School Division, "History" http://www.frontiersd.mb.ca/governance/policy/SitePages/History.aspx (accessed 3 August 2012).

26. Alberta Education, *The Northland School Division Inquiry*, 22, 30–31.

The students speak

1. Angie Crerar, quoted in Métis Nation, *Métis Memories*, 125.

2. Theresa Meltenberger, quoted in Métis Nation, *Métis Memories*, 27.

3. Elmer Cardinal, quoted in Métis Nation, *Métis Memories*, 72–74.

4. Alphonse Janvier, quoted in Métis Nation, *Métis Memories*, 19.

5. TRC, AVS, Robert Derocher, Statement to the Truth and Reconciliation Commission of Canada, Saskatoon, Saskatchewan, 21 June 2012, Statement Number: 2011-4380.

6. Theresa Meltenberger, quoted in Métis Nation, *Métis Memories*, 27.

7. Arcand, quoted in "Les Metisse," part 2, http://www.jkcc.com/motherstwo.html (accessed 1 January 2012).

8. Arcand, quoted in "Les Metisse," part 2, http://www.jkcc.com/motherstwo.html (accessed 1 January 2012).

9. Anonymous, quoted in Métis Nation, *Métis Memories*, 120.

10. James Thomas, quoted in Métis Nation, *Métis Memories*, 86.

11. Martha Mercredi, quoted in Métis Nation, *Métis Memories*, 91.

12. Magee Shaw, quoted in Métis Nation, *Métis Memories*, 7.

13. Anonymous, quoted in Métis Nation, *Métis Memories*, 13.

14. Anonymous, quoted in Métis Nation, *Métis Memories*, 15.

15. Anonymous, quoted in Métis Nation, *Métis Memories*, 122.

16. Anonymous, quoted in Métis Nation, *Métis Memories*, 61.

17. Rita Evans, quoted in Métis Nation, *Métis Memories*, 101.

18. Rita Evans, quoted in Métis Nation, *Métis Memories*, 103.

19. Colin Courtoreille, quoted in Métis Nation, *Métis Memories*, 49–50.

20. [Mike J. Durocher,] "Sandy Point," http://metis.tripod.com/Sandy.html (accessed 3 January 2012).

21. Anonymous, quoted in Métis Nation, *Métis Memories,* 39.

22. George Amato, quoted in Métis Nation, *Métis Memories,* 66.

23. Anonymous, quoted in Métis Nation, *Métis Memories,* 116.

24. TRC, AVS, Robert Derocher, Statement to the Truth and Reconciliation Commission of Canada, Saskatoon, Saskatchewan, 21 June 2012, Statement Number: 2011-4380.

25. Magee Shaw, quoted in Métis Nation, *Métis Memories,* 7.

26. "Ex-residential School Students Recall Painful Days," http://www.canada.com/topics/news/national/story.html?id=3ffcd4f0-9d28-4622-8768-7295d5c6bf80.

27. Alphonse Janvier, quoted in Métis Nation, *Métis Memories,* 20, 22.

28. TRC, AVS, Allen Morin, Statement to the Truth and Reconciliation Commission of Canada, Batoche, Saskatchewan, 19 July 2010, Statement Number: 01-SK-18-25JY10-002.

29. Anonymous, quoted in Chartrand, "Métis Residential School Participation," 21.

30. "Ex-residential School Students Recall Painful Days," http://www.canada.com/topics/news/national/story.html?id=3ffcd4f0-9d28-4622-8768-7295d5c6bf80; Clement Chartier, quoted in Kennedy, "News and Comment," 11 May 2006, Turtle Island Native Network, http://www.turtleisland.org/discussion/viewtopic.php?p=6938 (accessed 26 December 2011); "President Chartier Attends TRC Event in Inuvik, NWT," http://www.metisnation.ca/index.php/news/trc-event-in-nwt.

31. Durocher, "Sandy Point," http://metis.tripod.com/Sandy.html (accessed 3 January 2012).

32. TRC, AVS, Robert Derocher, Statement to the Truth and Reconciliation Commission of Canada, Saskatoon, Saskatchewan, 21 June 2012, Statement Number: 2011-4380.

33. George Amato, quoted in Métis Nation, *Métis Memories,* 67.

34. Anonymous, quoted in Métis Nation, *Métis Memories,* 42.

35. Colin Courtoreille, quoted in Métis Nation, *Métis Memories,* 49.

36. Donna Roberts, quoted in Métis Nation, *Métis Memories,* 52.

37. Anonymous, quoted in Métis Nation, *Métis Memories,* 116–117.

38. Elmer Cardinal, quoted in Métis Nation, *Métis Memories,* 74.

39. Anonymous, quoted in Logan, "Lost Generations," 80.

40. Pennier, *'Call Me Hank,'* 9–10, 13.

41. Archie Larocque, quoted in Métis Nation, *Métis Memories,* 35, 36.

42. oUR Space: Interview: Mrs. Mary Jacobson, Saskatchewan Archives Board, Sound Archives Programme: tape no. IH-132, transcript disc 23, interview with Mary Jacobson, conducted by Carol Pearlstone, 3 August 1973, transcribed by J. Greenwood. 1–12, http://ourspace.uregina.ca/ (accessed 6 November 2014).

43. Theresa Meltenberger, quoted in Métis Nation, *Métis Memories,* 28.

44. Theresa Meltenberger, quoted in Métis Nation, *Métis Memories,* 30.

45. Anonymous, quoted in Métis Nation, *Métis Memories,* 121.

46. Donna Roberts, quoted in Métis Nation, *Métis Memories,* 53.

47. Angie Crerar, quoted in Métis Nation, *Métis Memories,* 126.

48. Anonymous, quoted in Métis Nation, *Métis Memories,* 61.

49. Anonymous, quoted in Métis Nation, *Métis Memories,* 108.

50. "Vandale: R-805A," cited in Logan, "Lost Generations," 80.

51. Nungak, "Part Qallunaaq," http://www.electriccanadian.com/history/first/zebedee/index.htm (accessed 5 March 2012).

52. Dickson, *Hey, Monias!,* 86–87.

53. Dickson, *Hey, Monias!,* 93.

54. Alphonse Janvier, quoted in Métis Nation, *Métis Memories,* 23.

55. Anonymous, quoted in Métis Nation, *Métis Memories,* 83.

56. Alphonse Janvier, quoted in Métis Nation, *Métis Memories,* 20.

57. Anonymous, quoted in Métis Nation, *Métis Memories,* 38.

58. Magee Shaw, quoted in Métis Nation, *Métis Memories,* 8.

59. George Amato, quoted in Métis Nation, *Métis Memories,* 65.

60. Martha Mercredi, quoted in Métis Nation, *Métis Memories,* 91.

61. Arcand, quoted in "Les Metisse," part 2, http://www.jkcc.com/motherstwo.html (accessed 1 January 2012).

Bibliography

Primary Sources

1. Truth and Reconciliation Commission Databases

The endnotes of this report often commence with the abbreviation TRC, followed by one of the following abbreviations: ASAGR, AVS, CAR, IRSSA, NRA, RBS, and LAC. The documents so cited are located in the Truth and Reconciliation Commission of Canada's database, housed at the National Centre for Truth and Reconciliation. At the end of each of these endnotes, in square brackets, is the document identification number for each of these documents. The following is a brief description of each database.

Active and Semi-Active Government Records (ASAGR) Database: The Active and Semi-Active Government Records database contains active and semi-active records collected from federal governmental departments that potentially intersected with the administration and management of the residential school system. Documents that were relevant to the history and/or legacy of the system were disclosed to the Truth and Reconciliation Commission of Canada (TRC) in keeping with the federal government's obligations in relation to the Indian Residential Schools Settlement Agreement (IRSSA). Some of the other federal government departments included, but were not limited to, the Department of Justice, Health Canada, the Royal Canadian Mounted Police, and National Defence. Aboriginal Affairs and Northern Development Canada undertook the responsibility of centrally collecting and producing the records from these other federal departments to the TRC.

Audio/Video Statement (AVS) Database: The Audio/Video Statement database contains video and audio statements provided to the TRC at community hearings and regional and national events held by the TRC, as well as at other special events attended by the TRC.

Church Archival Records (CAR) Database: The Church Archival Records database contains records collected from the different church/religious entities that were involved in administration and management of residential schools. The church/religious entities primarily included, but were not limited to, entities associated with the Roman Catholic Church, the Anglican Church of Canada, the Presbyterian Church in Canada, and the United Church of Canada. The records were collected as part of the TRC's mandate, as set out in the Indian Residential Schools Settlement Agreement, to "identify sources and create as complete an historical record as possible of the IRS system and legacy."

Indian Residential Schools School Authority (IRSSA) Database: The Indian Residential Schools School Authority database is comprised of individual records related to each residential school, as set out by the IRSSA.

National Research and Analysis (NRA) Database: The National Research and Analysis database contains records collected by the National Research and Analysis Directorate, Aboriginal Affairs and Northern Development Canada, formerly Indian Residential Schools Resolution Canada (IRSRC). The records in the database were originally collected for the purpose of research into a variety of allegations, such as abuse in residential schools, and primarily resulted from court processes such as civil and criminal litigation, and later the Indian Residential Schools Settlement Agreement (IRSSA), as well as from out-of-court processes such as Alternative Dispute Resolution. A majority of the records were collected from Aboriginal Affairs and Northern Development Canada. The collection also contains records from other federal departments and religious entities. In the case of some records in the database that were provided by outside entities, the information in the database is incomplete. In those instances, the endnotes in the report reads, "No document location, no document file source."

Red, Black and School Series (RBS) Database: The Red, Black and School Series database contains records provided by Library and Archives Canada to the TRC. These three sub-series contain records that were originally part of the "Headquarters Central Registry System," or records management system, for departments that preceded the current federal department of Aboriginal Affairs and Northern Development Canada. The archival records are currently related to the Department of Indian Affairs and Northern Development fonds and are held as part of Library and Archives Canada's collection.

Library and Archives Canada (LACAR) Archival Records Container (File) and Document Databases – The LAC Records Container (File) and Document databases contain records collected from Library and Archives Canada (LAC). The archival records of federal governmental departments that potentially intersected with the administration and management of Indian Residential Schools were held as part of Library and Archives Canada's collection. Documents that were relevant to the history and/or legacy of the Indian Residential School system were initially collected by the Truth and Reconciliation Commission, in conjunction with Aboriginal Affairs and Northern Development Canada, as part of their mandate, as set out in the Indian Residential Schools Settlement Agreement. The collection of records was later continued by Aboriginal Affairs and Northern Development Canada, based on federal government's obligation to disclose documents in relation to the Indian Residential Schools Settlement Agreement.

2. Indian Affairs Annual Reports, 1864–1997

Within this report, *Annual Report of the Department of Indian Affairs* denotes the published annual reports created by the Government of Canada, and relating to Indian Affairs over the period from 1864 to 1997.

The Department of Indian Affairs and Northern Development was created in 1966. In 2011, it was renamed Aboriginal Affairs and Northern Development. Before 1966, different departments were responsible for the portfolios of Indian Affairs and Northern Affairs.

The departments responsible for Indian Affairs were (in chronological order):

- The Department of the Secretary of State of Canada (to 1869)
- The Department of the Secretary of State for the Provinces (1869–1873)
- The Department of the Interior (1873–1880)
- The Department of Indian Affairs (1880–1936)
- The Department of Mines and Resources (1936–1950)
- The Department of Citizenship and Immigration (1950–1965)
- The Department of Northern Affairs and National Resources (1966)
- The Department of Indian Affairs and Northern Development (1966 to the present)

The exact titles of Indian Affairs annual reports changed over time, and were named for the department.

3. Library and Archives Canada

RG10 (Indian Affairs Records Group) The records of RG10 at Library and Archives Canada are currently part of the R216, Department of Indian Affairs and Northern Development fonds. For clarity and brevity, in endnotes throughout this report, records belonging to the RG10 record group have been identified simply with their RG10 information.

Where a copy of an RG10 document held in a TRC database was used, the TRC database holding that copy is clearly identified, along with the RG10 information connected with the original document.

RG15 (Department of the Interior)

4. Other Archives

Oblates of Mary Immaculate Lacombe Canada, Grandin Province Archives

oUR Space (University of Regina's DSpace)

5. Government Publications

Alberta. Education. "The Northland School Division Inquiry Team report to the Honourable Dave Hancock, Minister of Education." Edmonton: Government of Alberta, 2010.

Canada. *Sessional Papers of the Dominion of Canada*, vol. 13, third session of the fifth Parliament, 1885.

Davin, N.F. *Report on Industrial Schools for Indians and Half-Breeds, to the Right Honourable the Minister of the Interior*. Ottawa: 1879.

Ewing, Albert Freeman. *Report of the Royal Commission Appointed to Investigate the Conditions of the Half-Breed Population of Alberta*. Edmonton, Government of Alberta, Department of Lands and Mines, 1936.

Howe, Joseph. "Statement of the condition of the various Indian Schools within the Dominion of Canada, derived from the latest Reports received at this Office." In *Report of the Indian Branch of the Secretary of State for the Provinces*. Ottawa: I.B. Taylor, 1872.

Voorhis, Ernest, editor. *Historic forts and trading posts of the French regime and of the English fur trading companies*. Ottawa: Department of the Interior, National Development Bureau, 1930.

Secondary Sources

1. Books and Published Reports

Andrew, Sheila Muriel. *The Development of Elites in Acadian New Brunswick, 1861–1881*. Montreal and Kingston: McGill-Queen's University Press, 1996.

Barron, Laurie F. *Walking in Indian Moccasins: The Native Policies of Tommy Douglas and the CCF*. Vancouver: University of British Columbia Press, 1997.

Bird, Madeline, with the assistance of Sister Agnes Sutherland. *Living Kindness: The Dream of My Life, The Memoirs of Metis Elder, Madeline Bird*. Yellowknife: Outcrop, 1991.

Blakeney, Allan. *An Honourable Calling: Political Memoirs*. Toronto: University of Toronto Press, 2008.

Blum, Rony. *Ghost Brothers: Adoption of a French Tribe by Bereaved Native America*. Montreal and Kingston: McGill-Queen's University Press, 2005.

Brown, Jennifer S.H. *Strangers in Blood: Fur Trade Company Families in Indian Country*. Vancouver: University of British Columbia Press, 1980.

Bumstead, J.M. *Canada's Diverse Peoples: A Reference Sourcebook*. Santa Barbara CA: ABC-CLIO, 2003.

Bumstead, J.M. *St. John's College: Faith and Education in Western Canada*. Winnipeg: University of Manitoba Press, 2006.

Campbell, Maria. *Halfbreed*. Toronto: McClelland and Stewart Limited, 1973.

Champagne, Joseph-Étienne. *Les missions catholiques dans l'ouest canadien, 1818–1875*. Ottawa: Éditions des Études oblates; Éditions de l'Université, 1949.

Chartrand, Larry N., Tricia E. Logan, and Judy D. Daniels. *Métis History and Experience and Residential Schools in Canada.* Prepared for the Aboriginal Healing Foundation Research Series, 2006.

Coates, Kenneth, and William Robert Morrison. *Land of the Midnight Sun: A History of the Yukon.* Montreal: McGill-Queen's University Press, 2005.

Curtis, Bruce. *The Politics of Population: State Formation, Statistics, and the Census of Canada, 1840–1875.* Toronto: University of Toronto Press, 2001.

Dempsey, Hugh A. *The Gentle Persuader: A Biography of James Gladstone, Indian Senator.* Saskatoon: Western Producer Books, 1986.

Devine, Heather. *The People Who Own Themselves: Aboriginal Ethnogenesis in a Canadian Family, 1660–1900.* Calgary: University of Calgary Press, 2004.

Dickerson, Mark O. *Whose North? Political Change, Political Development, and Self-Government in the Northwest Territories.* Vancouver: University of British Columbia Press and The Arctic Institute of North America, 1992.

Dickson, Stewart. *Hey, Monias! The Story of Raphael Ironstand.* Vancouver: Arsenal Pulp Press, 1993.

Dobbin, Murray. *The One and a Half Men: The Story of Jim Brady and Malcolm Norris, Métis Patriots of the Twentieth Century.* Vancouver: New Star Books, 1981.

Drouin, Eméric O. *Joyau dans la plaine; Saint-Paul, Alberta, colonie métisse 1896–1909, paroisse blanche 1909–1951.* Québec: Éditions Ferland, 1968.

Dugas, G. *Monseigneur Provencher et les missions de la Rivière-Rouge.* Montreal: O. Beauchemin & Fils, 1889.

Fumoleau, René. *As Long as This Land Shall Last: A History of Treaty 8 and Treaty 11, 1870–1939.* Calgary: University of Calgary Press, 2004.

Garrioch, Alfred Campbell. *The Far and Furry North: A Story of Life and Love and Travel in the Days of the Hudson's Bay Company.* Winnipeg: Douglas-McIntyre, 1925.

Huel, Raymond J.A. *Proclaiming the Gospel to the Indians and the Métis.* Edmonton: University of Alberta Press and Western Canadian Publishers, 1996.

Levin, Claire. *The Unheard Majority: A History of Women Educators in Manitoba.* Winnipeg: Manitoba Women's Directorate, 2002.

Marmon, Lee. "Final Report on Metis Education and Boarding School Literature and Sources Review." Prepared for the Métis National Council, February 2010.

McCarthy, Martha. *From the Great River to the Ends of the Earth: Oblate Missions to the Dene, 1847–1921.* Edmonton: University of Alberta Press, Western Canadian Publishers, 1995.

Metis Association of Alberta, Joe Sawchuk, Patricia Sawchuk, and Theresa Ferguson. *Metis Land Rights in Alberta: A Political History.* Edmonton: Metis Association of Alberta, 1981.

Métis Nation of Alberta. *Métis Memories of Residential Schools: A Testament to the Strength of the Métis.* Edmonton: Métis Nation of Alberta, 2004.

Moine, Louise. *My Life in a Residential School.* Saskatchewan: Provincial Chapter International Order of Daughters of the Empire, Saskatchewan, in Cooperation with the Provincial Library of Saskatchewan, 1975.

Peake, Frank. *The Bishop Who Ate His Boots: A Biography of Isaac O. Stringer.* Toronto: The Anglican Church of Canada, 1966.

Pennier, Henry. *'Call Me Hank': A Stó:lo Man's Reflections on Logging, Living, and Growing Old.* Edited by Keith Thor Carlson and Kristina Fagan. Toronto: University of Toronto Press, 2006.

Pocklington, T.C. *The Government and Politics of the Alberta Metis Settlements.* Regina: Canadian Plains Research Center, 1991.

Quiring, David M. *CCF Colonialism in Northern Saskatchewan: Battling Parish Priests, Bootleggers and Fur Sharks.* Vancouver: University of British Columbia Press, 2004.

Reimer, Gwen, and Jean-Philippe Chartrand. "A Historical Profile of the James Bay Area's Mixed European-Indian or Mixed European-Inuit Community." Prepared for Department of Justice, Canada, 14 March 2005.

Shortt, Adam, and Arthur George Doughty, editors. *Canada and its Provinces; A History of the Canadian People and Their Institutions.* Toronto: Publishers' Association of Canada, 1914.

Siggins, Maggie. *Riel: A Life of Revolution.* Toronto: HarperCollins, 1994.

West, James. *The substance of a journal during a residence at the Red River colony, British North America; and frequent excursions among the North-west American Indians, in the years 1820, 1821, 1822, 1823.* London: L.B. Seelev and Son, 1824.

Widder, Keith R. *Battle for the Soul: Métis Children Encounter Evangelical Protestants at Mackinaw Mission, 1823 1837.* East Lansing: Michigan State University Press, 1999.

Wilson, Daniel. *Prehistoric Man: Researches into the Origins of Civilisation in the Old and New World.* 3rd edition. London: Macmillan and Company, 1876.

2. Articles and Chapters in Books

Absolon, Kathy, and Cam Willett. "Putting Ourselves Forward: Location in Aboriginal Research." In *Research as Resistance: Critical, Indigenous and Anti-oppressive Approaches*, edited by Leslie Brown and Susan Strega, 97–126. Toronto: Scholar's Press, 2005.

Anuik, Jonathan. "Forming Civilization at Red River: 19th-century Missionary Education of Métis and First Nations Children." *Prairie Forum* 31, no. 1 (2006): 1–15.

Beaumont, Raymond M. "Origins and Influences: The Family Ties of the Reverend Henry Budd." *Prairie Forum* 17, no. 2 (1992): 167–200.

Beaumont, Raymond M. "The Rev. William Cockran: The Man and the Image." *Manitoba History* 33 (Spring 1997): 2–26.

Brown, Jennifer. "Fur Trade as Centrifuge: Familial Dispersal and Offspring Identity in Two Company Contexts." In *North American Indian Anthropology: Essays on Society and Culture*, edited by Raymond DeMallie and Alfonso Ortiz, 197–219. Norman: University of Oklahoma Press, 1994.

Carney, Robert. "Residential Schooling at Fort Chipewyan and Fort Resolution 1874–1974." In *Western Oblate Studies 2, Proceedings of the Second Symposium on the History of the Oblates in Western and Northern Canada,* edited by R.[-J.-A.] Huel with Guy Lacombe, 115–138. Lewiston, New York: Edwin Mellen Press, 1992.

Chalmers, J.W. "Northland: The Founding of a Wilderness School System." *Canadian Journal of Native Education* 12, no. 2 (1985): 1–45.

Chartrand, Larry N. "Métis Residential School Participation: A Literature Review." In *Métis History and Experience and Residential Schools in Canada*, by Larry N. Chartrand, Tricia E. Logan, and Judy D. Daniels, 5–55. Ottawa: Aboriginal Healing Foundation, 2006.

Church of England Sunday School Magazine for Teachers 6, new ser. (1862).

Coates, Kenneth. "'Betwixt and between': The Anglican Church and the Children of the Carcross (Choutla) Residential School, 1911–1954." In *Interpreting Canada's North: Selected*

Readings, edited by Kenneth Coates and William R. Morrison, 150–168. Toronto: Copp Clark Limited, 1989.

Comeau, Lisa. "Contemporary Productions of Colonial Identities through Liberal Discourses of Education Reform." *Journal of the Canadian Association for Curriculum Studies* 3, no. 2 (2005): 9–25.

Daniels, Judy D. "Ancestral Pain: Métis Memories of Residential School Project." Originally prepared for the Métis Nation of Alberta, 3 April 2003. In *Métis History and Experience and Residential Schools in Canada*, by Larry N. Chartrand, Tricia E. Logan, and Judy D. Daniels, 96–194. Ottawa: Aboriginal Healing Foundation, 2006.

Ens, Richard A. "'But What Is The Object of Educating These Children, If It Costs Their Lives to Educate Them?': Federal Indian Education Policy in Western Canada in the Late 1800s." *Journal of Canadian Studies/Revue d'études canadiennes* 43, no. 3 (2009): 101–123.

Erickson, Lesley A. "'Bury Our Sorrows in the Sacred Heart': Gender and the Métis Response to Colonialism—The Case of Sara and Louis Riel, 1848–83." In *Unsettled Pasts: Reconceiving the West through Women's History*, edited by Sarah Carter, Lesley Erickson, Patricia Roome, and Char Smith, 17–48. Calgary: University of Calgary Press, 2005.

Erickson, Lesley A. "Repositioning the Missionary: Sara Riel, the Grey Nuns, and Aboriginal Women in Catholic Missions of the Northwest." In *Recollecting: Lives of Aboriginal Women of the Canadian Northwest and Borderlands*, edited by Sarah Carter and Patricia McCormack, 115–134. Edmonton: Athabasca University Press, 2010.

Gladstone, James. "Indian School Days." *Alberta Historical Review* 15, no. 1 (1967): 18–24.

Jaenen, Cornelius J. "Foundations of Dual Education at Red River, 1811–34." *Transactions of the Historical and Scientific Society of Manitoba*, series III, 21 (1964–65): 35–68.

Logan, Tricia E. "Lost Generations: The Silent Métis of the Residential School System. Revised Interim Report." Originally prepared for Southwest Region of Manitoba Métis Federation, 2001. In *Métis History and Experience and Residential Schools in Canada*, by Larry N. Chartrand, Tricia E. Logan, and Judy D. Daniels, 57–93. Ottawa: Aboriginal Healing Foundation, 2006.

Long, John S. "Archdeacon Thomas Vincent of Moosonee and the Handicap of 'Métis' Racial Status." *Canadian Journal of Native Studies* 3 (1983): 95–116.

Long, John S. "Reviews: Other Media." *American Indian Culture and Research Journal, Special Métis Issue* 6, no. 2 (1982): 273–276.

Martin, Fred V. "Alberta Métis Settlements: A Brief History." In *Forging Alberta's Constitutional Framework*, edited by Richard Connors and John M. Law, 345–389. Edmonton: University of Alberta Press in association with the Centre for Constitutional Studies/Centre d'études constitionelles, 2005.

McGuire, Rita. "The Grey Sisters in the Red River Settlement, 1844-1870." *Canadian Catholic Historical Association Historical Studies* 53 (1986): 21–37.

Mumford, Jeremy. "*Mixed-Race Identity in a Nineteenth-Century Family: The Schoolcrafts of Sault Ste. Marie, 1824–27.*" *Michigan Historical Review* 25, no. 1 (1999): 1–23.

Ormiston, Alice. "Educating 'Indians': Practices of Becoming Canadian." *Canadian Journal of Native Studies* 22, no. 1 (2002): 1–22.

Prud'homme, Maurice. "The Life and Times of Archbishop Taché." Manitoba Historical Society *Transactions*, series 3 (1954–1955): 4–17.

Reardon, James M. "George Anthony Belcourt Pioneer Missionary of the Northwest." *Canadian Catholic Historical Association Report* 18 (1951): 75–89.

Reimer, Gwen, and Jean-Philippe Chartrand. "Documenting Historic Métis in Ontario." *Ethnohistory* 51, no. 3 (2004): 567–607.

Stanley, George F.G. "Alberta's Half-Breed Reserve Saint-Paul-des Métis 1896–1909." In *The Other Natives: The Metis,* vol. 2, edited by A.S. Lussier, and D.B. Sealey, 75–107. Winnipeg: Manitoba Metis Federation Press, 1978.

Stevenson, Mark. "Section 91 (24) and Canada's Legislative Jurisdiction with Respect to the Métis." *Indigenous Law Journal* 1 (Spring 2002): 238–261.

Stevenson, Winona. "The Journals and Voices of a Church of England Native Catechist: Askenootow (Charles Pratt), 1851–1884." In *Reading Beyond Words: Contexts for Native History*, edited by Jennifer S. H. Brown and Elizabeth Vibert, 304–329. Peterborough: Broadview Press, 1996.

Stevenson, Winona. "The Red River Indian Mission School and John West's 'Little Charges' 1820–1833." *Native Studies Review* 4, nos. 1 and 2 (1988): 129–165.

Tanner, Adrian. "The Aboriginal Peoples of Newfoundland and Labrador and Confederation." *Newfoundland Studies* 14, no. 2 (1998): 238–252.

Titley, E. Brian. "Dunbow Indian Industrial School: An Oblate Experiment in Education." In *Western Oblate Studies 2, proceedings of the second symposium on the history of the Oblates in western and northern Canada*, edited by R.[-J.-A.] Huel, with Guy Lacombe, 95–113. Lewiston, New York: Edwin Mellen Press, 1992.

Valentine, Victor F. "The Fort Black Co-operative Store: A Social Experiment Among the Ile a La Crosse Métis." In *A Different Drummer: Readings in Anthropology with a Canadian Perspective*, edited by Bruce Alden Cox, Jacques M. Chevalier, and Valda Blundell, 81–90. Ottawa: BCP Enterprises, 1989.

Van West, Carroll. "Acculturation by Design—Architectural Determinism and the Montana Indian Reservations, 1870–1930." *Great Plains Quarterly* 7 (Spring 1987): 91–102.

3. Theses and Dissertations

Boyd, Diane Michelle. "The Rise and Development of Female Catholic Education in the Nineteenth-Century Red River Region: The Case of Catherine Mulaire." Master of Arts thesis, Department of History, Joint Master's Program, Universities of Manitoba and Winnipeg, 1999.

Carney, Robert. "Relations in Education Between the Federal and Territorial Governments and the Roman Catholic Church in the Mackenzie District, Northwest Territories, 1867–1961." PhD dissertation, University of Alberta, 1971.

Foran, Timothy Paul. "Les Gens de Cette Place: Oblates and the Evolving Concept of *Métis* at Île-à-la-Crosse, 1845–1898." PhD dissertation, University of Ottawa, 2011.

Fox, Uta. "The Failure of the Red Deer Industrial School." Master of Arts thesis, University of Calgary, 1993.

Gresko, Jacqueline Kennedy. "Gender and Mission: The Founding Generations of the Sisters of Saint Ann and the Oblates of Mary Immaculate in British Columbia 1858–1914." PhD dissertation, University of British Columbia, 1999.

Logan, Tricia Elizabeth. "We Were Outsiders: The Metis and Residential Schools." Master of Arts thesis, University of Manitoba, 2007.

Malloy, Margaret, "The History of St. Mary's Academy and College and Its Times." Master of Education thesis, University of Manitoba, 1952.

Marceau-Kozicki, Sylvie. "Onion Lake Residential Schools, 1893–1943." Master of Arts thesis, University of Saskatchewan, 1993.

Redford, James W. "Attendance at Indian Residential Schools in British Columbia, 1890-1920." Master of Arts thesis, University of British Columbia, 1978.

Stevenson Winona L. "The Church Missionary Society Red River Mission and the Emergence of a Native Ministry 1820–1860, with a Case Study of Charles Pratt of Touchwood Hills." Master of Arts thesis, University of British Columbia, 1988.

4. Online Sources

"Alberta Métis Settlements." DWRG Press. http://www.ualberta.ca/~walld/ab2introsketch. html (accessed 23 March 2012).

Allaire, Gratien. "Chaboillez, Charles." In *Dictionary of Canadian Biography* Online. http://www.biographi.ca/en/bio/chaboillez_charles_5E.html (accessed 30 November 2011).

Anglican Church of Canada. Mission and Justice Relationships, Truth and Reconciliation. "Bishop Horden Memorial School–Moose Factory Island, ON." http://www.anglican.ca/relationships/trc/histories/bishop-horden/ (accessed 10 December 2014).

Anglican Church of Canada. Mission and Justice Relationships, Truth and Reconciliation. "Bishop Horden Memorial School–Moose Factory Island, ON." http://www.anglican.ca/relationships/trc/histories/bishop-horden/ (accessed 21 October 2011).

Armour, David A. "Henry, Alexander." In *Dictionary of Canadian Biography* Online. http://www.biographi.ca/en/bio/henry_alexander_1739_1824_6E.html (accessed 30 December 2011).

[Ausland, Selmer.] "Arrival of the Grey Nuns: The First Schools and the Boarding School." http://www.jkcc.com/rcnuns.html (accessed 23 December 2011).

[Ausland, Selmer.] "Chateau Saint-Jean ... Black Robes and Grey Dresses." Part 1. http://www.jkcc.com/robes.html (accessed 1 January 2012).

[Ausland, Selmer.] "Hospital Buildings and Health Care." http://www.jkcc.com/rchospital. html (accessed 6 January 2012).

[Ausland, Selmer.] "Ile-A-La-Crosse celebrates Bi-Centennial, Courtesy of 'DENOSA.'" http://www.jkcc.com/invaintwo.html (accessed 6 January 2012).

[Ausland, Selmer.] "Les Metisse... Mothers and Grandmothers." Part 2. http://www.jkcc.com/motherstwo.html (accessed 1 January 2012).

[Ausland, Selmer.] "Memories of Deep River Website. Religious History of St. John Baptiste Parish, Ile-A-La-Crosse, 150 Years." http://www.jkcc.com/rcindex.html (accessed 10 December 2014).

[Ausland, Selmer.] "Today ... We Have Not Lived In Vain." Part 2. http://www.jkcc.com/invaintwo.html (accessed 6 January 2012).

Barkwell, Lawrence. "Anne Goulet (1842–1917)." Louis Riel Institute. http://www.scribd.com/doc/56460013/Sister-Anne-Goulet (accessed 26 January 2012).

Barkwell, Lawrence. "Mary Jane McDougall (1844–1896)." Louis Riel Institute. http://www.scribd.com/doc/32469225/Sister-Mary-Jane-McDougall-Grey-Nun (accessed 26 January 2012).

Barkwell, Lawrence. "Napoleon Laferté, O.M.I. (1896–1964)." Louis Riel Institute. http://www.scribd.com/doc/32835056/Father-Napoleon-Lafferty (accessed 26 January 2012).

Barkwell, Lawrence. "The Metis Homeland: Its Settlements and Communities." Louis Riel Institute. http://www.scribd.com/doc/26282327/Metis-Settlements-and-Communities (accessed 5 March 2012).

Bonin, Marie. "The Grey Nuns and the Red River Settlement." *Manitoba History* 11 (Spring 1986). http://www.mhs.mb.ca/docs/mb_history/11/greynuns.shtml (accessed 24 January 2012).

Boon, T.C. "Budd, Henry." In *Dictionary of Canadian Biography* Online. http://www.biographi.ca/en/bio/budd_henry_10E.html (accessed 5 December 2011).

Brown, "Metis." In *The Canadian Encyclopedia*. Institut Historica/Dominion Institute. http://www.thecanadianencyclopedia.ca/en/article/metis/ (accessed 8 December 2014).

Chartier, Clement. "President Chartier attends TRC event in Inuvik, NWT." http://www.metisnation.ca/index.php/news/trc-event-in-nwt.

Chaput, Donald. "Nolin, Jean-Baptiste." In *Dictionary of Canadian Biography* Online. http://www.biographi.ca/en/bio/nolin_jean_baptiste_1826_6E.html (accessed 14 January 2012).

Cyr, Jean-Roch. "Landry, Sir Pierre-Amand." In *Dictionary of Canadian Biography* Online. http://www.biographi.ca/en/bio/landry_pierre_amand_14E.html (accessed 8 November 2011).

Dictionary of Newfoundland English Online. http://www.heritage.nf.ca/dictionary/.

Durocher, Mike J. "Sandy Point." http://metis.tripod.com/Sandy.html (accessed 3 January 2012).

Flanagan, Thomas. "Hugh Richardson." In *Dictionary of Canadian Biography* Online. http://www.biographi.ca/en/bio/richardson_hugh_1826_1913_14E.html (accessed 1 August 2012).

Fleury, Norm. "Norm Fleury (NF) Interview–Mary St. Pierre." http://www.metismuseum.ca/media/document.php/01194.pdf (accessed 18 March 2012).

Foster, J.E. "Auld, William." In *Dictionary of Canadian Biography* Online. http://biographi.ca/009004-119.01-e.php?id_nbr=2738 (accessed 24 December 2011).

Frontier School Division. "History." http://www.frontiersd.mb.ca/governance/policy/SitePages/History.aspx.

Graham, Angela. "Memorable Manitobans: Angelique Nolin (?–1869)." http://www.mhs.mb.ca/docs/people/nolin_a.shtml (accessed 14 January 2012).

Higgins, Jenny. "Grenfell Mission." Newfoundland and Labrador Heritage Website, 2008. http://www.heritage.nf.ca/society/grenfellmission.html (accessed 10 November 2011).

Higgins, Jenny. "Impact of Non-Aboriginal Activities on the Inuit." Newfoundland and Labrador Heritage Website, 2008. http://www.heritage.nf.ca/aboriginal/inuit_impacts.html (accessed 9 November 2011).

Higgins, Jenny. "Métis Organizations and Land Claims." Newfoundland and Labrador Heritage Website. http://www.heritage.nf.ca/aboriginal/metis_claims.html (accessed 12 January 2012).

Kennedy, Bob. "News and Comment." Turtle Island Native Network, 11 May 2006. http://www.turtleisland.org/discussion/viewtopic.php?p=6938 (accessed 26 December 2011).

Lemieux, Lucien. "Provencher, Joseph-Norbert." In *Dictionary of Canadian Biography* Online. http://www.biographi.ca/009004-119.01-e.php?BioId=38265 (accessed 14 January 2012).

Lindsay, Margaret Anne, and Jennifer S.H. Brown. "Memorable Manitobans: Mary Jane McDougall (1842–1896). http://www.mhs.mb.ca/docs/people/mcdougall_mj.shtml (accessed 28 September 2014).

Manitoba. Archives of Manitoba. Hudson's Bay Company Archives. "Beaulieu, Francois 'A'," biographical sheet. http://www.gov.mb.ca/chc/archives/hbca/biographical/b/beaulieu_francois.pdf (accessed 5 January 2012).

Manitoba. Archives of Manitoba. Hudson's Bay Company Archives. "Hope, James," biographical sheet. http://www.gov.mb.ca/chc/archives/hbca/biographical/h/hope_james.pdf (accessed 19 January 2012).

Manitoba. Archives of Manitoba. Hudson's Bay Company Archives. "McKenzie, Samuel," biographical sheet. http://www.gov.mb.ca/chc/archives/hbca/biographical/mc/mckenzie_samuel1827-1874.pdf (accessed 26 December 2011).

McLennan, David. "Ile-a-la-Crosse." *Encyclopedia of Saskatchewan*. http://esask.uregina.ca/entry/ile-a-la-crosse.html (accessed 22 December 2011).

Morton, W.L. "Riel, Louis." In *Dictionary of Canadian Biography* Online. http://www.biographi.ca/en/bio/riel_louis_1817_64_9E.html (accessed 26 December 2011).

Neatby, Leslie H. "Beaulieu, François." In *Dictionary of Canadian Biography* Online. http://www.biographi.ca/en/bio/beaulieu_francois_10E.html (accessed 28 December 2011).

Nicks, John. "Thompson, David." In *Dictionary of Canadian Biography* Online. http://www.biographi.ca/en/bio/thompson_david_1770_1857_8E.html (accessed 30 November 2011).

Nungak, Zebedee. "Part Qallunaaq: From Hudson Bay to the Firth of Tay: Searching for My Scottish Grandfather." http://www.electriccanadian.com/history/first/zebedee/index.htm (accessed 5 March 2012).

"St. Pierre, Mrs. Mary" (obituary). http://baileysfuneralhome.com/book-of-memories/1488588/Pierre-Mary/obituary.php?Printable=true (accessed 18 March 2012).

Racette, Sherry Farrell. "Métis Education." *Encyclopedia of Saskatchewan*. http://esask.uregina.ca/entry/metis_education.html (accessed 5 December 2011).

Saskatoon Star-Phoenix. "Ex-residential School Students Recall Painful Days." http://www.canada.com/topics/news/national/story.html?id=3ffcd4f0-9d28-4622-8768-7295d5c6bf80 (accessed 23 December 2011).

Smith, Donald B. "Onasakenrat (Onesakenarat), Joseph." In *Dictionary of Canadian Biography* Online. http://www.biographi.ca/en/bio/onasakenrat_joseph_11E.html (accessed 30 November 2011).

Thomas, Lewis G. "Settee, James." In *Dictionary of Canadian Biography* Online. http://www.biographi.ca/en/bio/settee_james_13E.html (accessed 9 December 2011).

Turner, C. "Economics, Credentials, and Our Educational Expectations." 12 April 2002. http://www.scribd.com/doc/111050/Policy-and-History-of-Education-in-Ontario (accessed 16 January 2012).

University of Manitoba. "History of St. John's College." http://umanitoba.ca/colleges/st_johns/anglican/index.html (accessed 8 March 2012).

Van Kirk, Sylvia. "Isbister, Alexander Kennedy." In *Dictionary of Canadian Biography* Online. http://www.biographi.ca/en/bio/isbister_alexander_kennedy_11E.html. (accessed 14 January 2012).

Wall, D. "Joseph Francis Dion." Canadian Aboriginal Issues Database. http://www.ualberta.ca/~walld/dion.html (accessed 23 March 2012).